50p

Delicious Desserts

Author: Annette Wolter
Photography: Rolf Feuz and Karin Messerli
Translated by UPS Translations, London
Edited by Josephine Bacon

CLB 4184
This edition published in 1995 by Colour Library Books Ltd
Published originally under the title "Desserts"
by Gräfe und Unzer Verlag GmbH, München
© 1995 Gräfe und Unzer Verlag GmbH, München
English translation copyright: © 1995 by
Colour Library Books Ltd, Godalming, Surrey
Typeset by Image Setting, Brighton, E. Sussex
Printed and bound in Singapore
All rights reserved
ISBN 1-85833-318-0

DELICIOUS DESSERTS

Annette Wolter

Contributors
Elke Alsen, Marieluise Christl-Licosa,
Marey Kurz, Hannelore Mähl-Strenge,
Bernd Schiansky and Brigitta Stuber

Photography
Rolf Feuz and Karin Messerli

CLB
Colour Library Books

Contents

About this Book
Page 6

The Value of Desserts
Page 7

How to Make Successful Desserts
Page 8-15

Decorating the Desserts
Page 14-15

A Dessert for Every Day of the Week
Page 16-41

Hot Puddings
Page 42-63

Classic Desserts

Page 64-85

Frozen Desserts

Page 86-117

Important Dessert Ingredients

Page 118-123

Making Ice Cream

Page 124-125

Index

Page 126-128

About this Book

Delicious desserts offer a magnificent climax to a successful meal and have always been the culinary highlight of festive menus as well as of everyday meals. The varied recipes in this book have been put together with great care and should provide the perfect recipe for every occasion. In developing recipe ideas, all the authors felt that one of their tasks was to use nutritionally valuable ingredients such as fresh fruit or dairy products, to keep them as natural as possible and to ensure that their cooking was as light as possible. Each recipe is easy to follow because it is described in an uncomplicated way. Each dish has been photographed in colour and provides the perfect guide to achieving a good result.

Before you get to the comprehensive recipe section you will find some step-by-step photographs in colour with accompanying text describing basic methods of preparation and cooking which are most often used for desserts. These include instructions on how to peel a pineapple properly and how to handle gelatine correctly. If you follow the instructions exactly, you will be able to create the most elaborate desserts. Stiffly beaten egg whites should shine like silk – just as they do in the helpful working photos. Home-made caramel is not such a complicated procedure thanks to the full description. Great new ideas for creating original toppings and decorations are shown in text and pictures.

The nutritional values given with each recipe show you how fattening the dessert is, in other words how many joules or calories it contains. In leafing through the pages of this book you will see that besides sumptuous feasts there are also wonderfully light creations such as Citrons Givrés, Melon and Peach Granités, various delicious sorbets, fruit ice creams and buttermilk jelly. All these desserts will round off a nutritious meal particularly well. However, if you want to spoil your family or friends with sweet pancakes, Viennese pancakes or delicious filled crêpes, perhaps you should just serve a hearty soup for the main course.

In order for you to plan the meal sensibly, the preparation and cooking times are shown. For instance, you will need to know the approximate times for recipes containing gelatine. Desserts which need to be kept chilled or frozen do have the advantage that they can be prepared well in advance and served at a time convenient to you.

The first chapter is entitled 'A Dessert for Every Day of the Week' and presents suggestions for desserts to supplement the daily menu throughout the entire year. Preparing these sweets does not involve very much work. The second chapter, 'Hot Puddings', is devoted to flambéed, browned and baked desserts. Naturally, classic desserts such as Charlotte Royale, Moor in a Shirt and Tiramisù have also been included. Last but not least, you will find 'Iced Desserts', dishes which you are unlikely to find at even the most exotic ice cream parlours or confectioners – these imaginative creations have to be made at home. The frosty parfaits, sorbets, granités and ice cream gateaux will delight the most demanding gourmet.

At the end of the book you will find valuable information on important dessert ingredients, on home-grown fruit, exotic fruit and aromatic spices. With 'Hot Tips for Iced Desserts', we go into the details of ice cream making and show you the utensils you can buy. And if you can't decide which dessert to try first, the extensive recipe and subject index at the end of the book will also help you to find the desired recipe quickly.

We hope you have lots of fun making and tasting all these exquisite desserts.

Unless otherwise stated, all recipes are calculated for four servings. The abbreviations 'kJ' and 'kCal' in the recipes indicate kilojoule and kilocalorie.

The Value of Desserts

Frequently the dessert is branded as a 'sweet sin'. Admittedly, many of the most popular desserts are not exactly low in calories, but because they are made with fresh fruit and dairy products they supply valuable nutrients and are a tasty ending to a meal. The 'sin' is to be found only in a lack of moderation. And for that you can hardly lay down binding rules.

Its Place in the Menu

The type and quantity of the dessert should always harmonise with the rest of a meal. The nutritional values given with each recipe are a useful planning aid for people who feel that calorie counting is important. Before deciding to give a particular dessert a miss, why not simply serve smaller portions. Or the main course could consist just of a light vegetable soup, a mixed salad or an hors d'oeuvre of fish or seafood, lean meat or poultry, and you could omit those calorie-rich trimmings. The recipes in this book have not been created under the motto of 'moderation in all things' but under the motto 'everything is permitted as long as it tastes good'. After all, the dessert is to be the crowning finish to a menu and definitely a reason for feasting.

Fresh Fruit

In addition to its actual enjoyment, fruit is of special importance for a balanced diet. It plays a major role in the case of desserts. It is usually eaten raw or is cooked as lightly as possible. We take it for granted that all fruit desserts have a season: in other words, fresh fruit grown outdoors locally is best used in season. However, many so-called exotic fruits are in the shops all year round. The experts agree that thanks to

modern harvesting and transport conditions a high percentage of nutrients are retained in exotic fruit.

Other Main Ingredients

Apart from fruit, dairy products such as yogurt, soft cheeses of all types, milk, cream and eggs are among the most frequent ingredients in desserts, irrespective of whether they are chilled, frozen as ice cream or sorbet, or served hot. Creamy desserts and ice creams are often based on an egg custard. Egg whites whisked until stiff and carefully folded into the mixture will guarantee a fine, light foamy texture. The eggs must be absolutely fresh so that the egg yolks can be cleanly separated from the whites. Traces of egg white in the yolk will become stringy when other liquids are added; yolk in the egg white will stop the whites from foaming into stiff peaks. Double cream should only be whipped just prior to using or serving. However, if whipped cream has to remain stiff for a long period, gelatine, being a natural product, is preferable to artificial stiffening agents.

Sugar and the Alternatives

Many of these dessert ideas are wholefood recipes, which goes to show that sweet things can still comply with the strict standards of modern nutrition. This book shows you that there is no difficulty in making traditional, famous and much loved desserts with sweeteners other than refined sugar. Large quantities of white sugar cannot be part of a healthy diet. However, there is little to say against sugar as a spice, in other words in moderate amounts. Acceptable alternatives to refined sugar in desserts include nutritionally more valuable sweeteners such as pure honey, maple syrup, molasses, treacle, concentrated apple or pear juice and raw cane sugars, such as Barbados sugar. The energy content (equivalent to the calorific value) of these unrefined sweeteners is not much less than that of refined sugar, but the minerals and vitamins which are important for the body's functions are contained in far greater amounts.

From the Full Grain

You will learn from the wholefood recipes in this book that even ordinary household flour can be replaced by nutritionally more valuable cereal products such as wholemeal flour. The most nutritious parts of the grain are in the germ and its husk. These are wheatgerm oil, proteins, almost all the vitamins in the B complex, vitamins D and E, as well as minerals and trace elements. Only the inner part of the grain is milled to make refined white flour.

The Gourmet Dessert

All in all, the value of a dessert is not determined by its ingredients alone but also to a large extent by the pleasant experience which enhances any occasion for eating and drinking. The most elaborate desserts, however, are not meant for every day. They should be kept for the rarer occasions for uninhibited enjoyment. Attractive decoration and toppings, including attractive presentations with fresh fruits, are especially important both for everyday and for special occasions.

How to Make Successful Desserts

Whipped egg white must shine

If a recipe requires stiffly-beaten egg white made stiffer and glossy by the addition of sugar, in other words meringue, follow these instructions and pictures. It is important that the egg white should be as cold as possible and the mixing bowl, the egg whisk or the electric mixer must be absolutely free of fat. When making a dessert, beat the egg white and refrigerate it before the egg-beater is used for other mixtures.

When separating the eggs, be careful to ensure that none of the yolk gets into the white. Hold the egg yolk over a bowl and slide it from one half of the shell to the other, using the thumb to remove the thread-like membrane that attaches the white to the shell. The egg white will drop into the bowl.

Treat whipped cream carefully

Like egg whites, whipped cream will lighten creams or fruit purées and will lend them a smooth consistency. Dots, rosettes or garlands of whipped cream piped onto foil can easily be frozen and can be used later as decoration for desserts and gâteaux. If whipped cream is to be sweetened using sugar, mix the sugar into the liquid cream so that it can dissolve during beating. Flavourings such as cocoa powder, instant coffee powder, syrup or liqueurs should be folded gradually into the stiff whipped cream in small quantities.

The cream, which should be as cold as possible, must be beaten with a whisk or an electric blender at medium speed until it begins to thicken. Then use the lowest speed until a stiff, firm, whipped cream results. On no account beat at top speed.

Caramelising – as easy as pie!

This popular aromatic sugar concentrate is frequently needed for special desserts. Caramel is used to coat fruits, line moulds or is spun in thin threads over a rolling pin to make 'angel's hair' as a decoration for delicate cream desserts.

The quantity of sugar given in the recipe should be brought to the boil in water, stirring until the sugar has dissolved completely. Reduce the heat and boil the syrup in a heavy based wide saucepan without stirring until at least half the water has evaporated and the syrup colours. It is important to use a good quality saucepan, because the heat must be distributed evenly to control the sugar temperature. A sugar thermometer is a very useful accessory.

Correct use of gelatine

Gelatine is a natural product with a neutral taste and is sold in the form of leaves or powder. A packet of powdered gelatine is equivalent to six leaves. Gelatine will always set if you keep to certain basic rules. The explanations and pictures should help to prevent mistakes.

Leaves of gelatine must be soaked in plenty of cold water until they are soft. Powdered gelatine should be soaked in a little cold water for at least five minutes, then heated very gently in the soaking water until it liquefies.

Whisk egg white with a pinch of salt, cream of tartar or lemon juice until stiff peaks form. If sugar is to be added, whisk the egg white until fluffy, then gradually add the sugar and continue whisking until stiff and glossy.

Spoon the meringue over the cream or pastry and fold it into the mixture with a mixing spoon until both are blended. Do not stir in the meringue as this would destroy the air bubbles and the lightening effect would be lost.

Either fold the whipped cream into the mixture as for egg whites or, if you are using it for decoration, use it to fill a piping bag fitted with a star nozzle. Hold the piping bag taut with one hand pressing over the whipped cream at the top of the bag, and the other hand guiding the nozzle like a pencil.

Stars, rosettes or garlands of cream can be made using a star nozzle of the right size. Dots can be made with a plain nozzle. Depending on the dessert, decorate the cream with berries or leaves and sprinkle with chopped nuts or dust with sieved cocoa powder.

The caramel must not be too dark because it would then taste bitter. To test for colour, allow some caramel to drip onto a white plate. Take the strong, honey-coloured caramel off the heat and use according to the recipe.

For crème caramel only the bottom of the mould is generally coated with caramel. In other desserts the moulds should be coated all over with it. To do this pour a little caramel into each mould and tip and twist it so that all the surfaces become coated.

Leaves of gelatine should be pressed out after soaking and dissolved in the hot liquid (on no account boiling), stirring all the time. Powdered gelatine which is already liquid should be handled in the same way. The slightly cooled dessert should be allowed to set in the refrigerator for between 30 minutes and four hours depending on the consistency desired.

In order to stiffen a cold liquid, cold purée or whipped cream, place the squeezed gelatine in a ladle and hold it in a pan of hot water to dissolve it. First mix the still warm gelatine with three tablespoons of the cold substance, then slowly mix in the whole quantity.

How to Make Successful Desserts

Segmenting citrus fruits

Segments of citrus fruits are often used as decoration for creams, sorbets and festive desserts. The fruit is first peeled then the flesh separated from the fine membranes which divide it into segments. This does take time, but is easy if these instructions are followed:

Peel the orange or grapefruit like an apple, using a sharp knife with a thin blade and making sure the pith is completely removed.

Fine juliennes

Matchstick strips of fruit, fruit peel (and vegetables) are called a julienne in French culinary terms. They are used for toppings and decoration, and at the same time provide a delightful aroma. For desserts, a julienne usually consists of strips of citrus zest and the best method of cutting julienne is shown here using a lemon.

First cut the peel lengthways from the washed lemon in 2cm/1-inch-wide strips. Then turn the strips over, hold them down and, using a sharp knife with a thin blade, carefully remove all traces of the white pith. If possible, the strips should remain whole.

Peeling a pineapple

Since relatively cheap, fresh pineapple is available almost the whole year round, tinned pineapple is becoming less and less popular. It has important uses, however, as fresh pineapple will not set in a jelly and can curdle a milky dessert because it contains an enzyme – bromelin – which affects protein. So, when making a pineapple jelly or creamy dessert, either use tinned pineapple or heat the pineapple first. Peeling a fresh pineapple is an art. Try using our suggestions shown in the text and pictures.

First cut off the leafy crown with a small piece of pineapple. Then peel off the tough skin, using a sharp knife.

Melon shells for decoration

Fruit shells make excellent containers for decorative desserts or salads. For festive occasions, it is well worth halving the fruits with a zig-zag cut as the serrated edge is particularly attractive. All citrus fruits are suitable for this purpose, but melons are particularly easy to use.

Wash the melons in warm water, dry and use the tip of a knife to trace a horizontal line around the middle. Holding the blade diagonally, pierce the fruit to the centre, then cut alternately upwards and downwards in an even zig-zag pattern. Pull the separated halves apart and scoop out the seeds.

Hold the whole fruit over a plate and, using a sharp knife with a thin blade, separate each segment from the membranes. You will have to test whether you find this easier while resting the fruit on a work surface or whether you prefer to hold the fruit in your hand.

Now carefully remove the fruit segments from the membranes and, if necessary, remove the pips with the knife. Depending on the intended use, take care that the segments remain whole. Squeeze the remaining membranes and use this, and any other excess juice, in the dessert.

With the shiny side uppermost, lay the strips of peel on a chopping board and cut lengthways into 1mm/-1/8 inch-wide julienne strips. All the strips should be of equal width; be careful not to tear them.

The julienne should be used as described in the recipe. For decoration, it is boiled in a sugar syrup for three to four minutes, to prevent it from drying out. It then resembles crystallised fruits, especially when coated with sifted icing sugar.

Using a large, sharp knife, and working diagonally downwards make V-shaped cuts into the pineapple to remove the 'eyes'. This produces an attractive indented edge. Cut the fruit into regular slices, about 1 cm/1/2 - inch thick.

Use a round cutter of about 3cm/1 1/4 inch diameter or a sharp knife to remove the woody core. Then use the slices as instructed in the recipe. Where appropriate in the recipe, use the leaf crown as decoration.

With a sharp-edged spoon, remove the seeds from the melon halves. Place them in a bowl and then press out in a sieve so that the fruit juice can be used in the dessert.

Use a melon baller, or a tea spoon, to remove the melon flesh from the halves. There should be about a 2cm/1-inch thick layer of flesh left in the shells. Unless they are to be served in bowls, cut a thin slice from the underside so that they do not overbalance.

How to Make Successful Desserts

The bain-marie

Some ingredients which are very sensitive to heat, such as egg yolk or gelatine, need to be heated in order to attain the correct consistency for some recipes. However, if heated too rapidly or for too long, egg yolk will coagulate and gelatine will not set. These ingredients need to be placed in a metal bowl which is a good conductor of heat, or a double boiler and then set over a pan of hot water; the bowl must not touch the bottom of the pan and the water should not be allowed to boil. This is known as a bain-marie or a water bath. If a hot mixture must be cooled rapidly, it should be placed in a pan of cold water containing plenty of ice cubes.

First have ready a double boiler, bain-marie or a saucepan of the right size to hold a metal basin. The basin should just touch the surface of the water but not sink too deeply into the saucepan. Alternatively use a small saucepan and hold it over a larger one.

Soufflé dishes and ramekins

Various types of large and small soufflé dishes, ramekins and dariole moulds are used for holding desserts. When purchasing, care should be taken that the moulds are ovenproof so they can be used for both hot and cold puddings. A good size for a ramekin or individual soufflé mould is 200ml/6 fl oz, even if it is not always filled to the brim. Tall, narrow moulds are recommended for hot soufflés, so the mixture will rise well during cooking.

Grease the moulds with butter, then sprinkle with caster sugar: put one tablespoon of sugar in the mould and turn in all directions until the sugar covers the inner surfaces. Shake out any excess sugar.

Unmoulding desserts

Puddings, jellies, creams or ice cream desserts often have to be unmoulded before serving. The dessert must be of a consistency that can be unmoulded, and this requires the use of stiffening agents such as gelatine or cornflour, or a combination of ingredients which set during cooking, such as a firm custard. The best way of turning out a dessert is shown in the adjacent pictures.

Allow a hot pudding to cool in the mould. Whether a dessert has to be turned out of a large mould or several small moulds, the first step is to run the tip of a thin, sharp knife round the edge of the mould to loosen the contents.

Flambéed desserts

When flambéed, desserts take on the tang of the alcohol. The flavour should be no stronger than that of the main ingredients of the dish. Calvados, brandy, kirsch, 40 percent proof rum or liqueurs and spirits with an alcohol content of no less than 38 percent proof can all be flamed. Flamed fruit, served on ice cream, looks most impressive, as do flambéed crêpes, beignets or rich, fruity puddings.

If you want to flame a dish at the table, you will need a rechaud, a table-top spirit stove – which consists of a special flaming pan and a sauce ladle. For desserts, a fruity sauce is boiled down in the pan with some sugar until it is syrupy.

Heat the water in the saucepan to nearly boiling, place the basin of mixture over it and then adjust the heat so that the water simmers gently. Continue stirring or whisking the mixture until it has reached the correct consistency. The water may only be allowed to come to the boil if the bowl does not actually touch it.

A double boiler or bain-marie are well suited for cooling the mixture. Here it is also important that none of the water gets into the mixture. The more ice cubes are added to the cold water, the quicker the mixture will cool.

If the moulds are likely to be too small or too shallow for the soufflé mixture, cut out strips of folded greaseproof paper wide enough to make them a good 4 cm/2 inches higher than the moulds when wrapped around them. Arrange the paper collars around the outside of the moulds and secure them with kitchen string. These collars are also used in the preparation of cold soufflés.

If you do not have enough moulds you can make some more from heavy-duty aluminium foil. Fold a large piece of foil and press around a mould. Tie it just below the rim with kitchen string. Press the edges of the foil outwards and carefully remove the mould.

To unmould ice cream, dip the mould into cold water; dip moulds holding desserts which have set in the refrigerator into warm water.

For large moulds, take the plate onto which the dessert is to be served and place it on top of the open mould. Then cover with a cloth and invert both quickly. Desserts in small moulds should be turned out straight onto individual dessert plates. If the dessert sticks or is likely to stick, wet the cloth with hot water.

In this sauce the fruits or crêpes to be flamed are heated, turned at least once and the sauce spooned over them. The alcohol to be used is slightly warmed in a ladle over a candle flame.

The alcohol is poured down the side of the pan and some is dribbled on to the ingredients to be flamed. The alcohol is ignited using a long match. It is allowed to burn for a short while then the flaming dessert is arranged on plates and coated with the sauce. Another way is to warm the alcohol in a saucepan in the kitchen, pour it into a warmed ladle, drizzle it over the pudding and set fire to it before quickly bringing it to the table.

Decorating the Dessert

Chocolate for decoration

Chocolate for decoration is on sale in the form of vermicelli (sprinkles), mocha-flavoured beans or chocolate flake or caraque.

1 To use a block of cooking or dessert chocolate for making strands, allow it to soften slightly until it is firm but pliable. Pare it into fine strips using a paring knife or vegetable peeler; the strips will disintegrate as if grated.

2 To make chocolate caraque or flakes, melt the chocolate in a basin over a pan of hot water or in a microwave oven. Spread it almost paper-thin onto a smooth, cool surface and scrape off after it solidifies.

3 To make chocolate leaves, melt the chocolate in a basin over a pan of hot water or in a microwave oven. Use a fine brush to paint the chocolate onto leaves that have been washed and dried and allow to set in the freezer for about 20 minutes. Peel the leaves away from the chocolate.

4 To make chocolate sauce, melt the chocolate with a little single cream mixed with diced, crystallised fruits.

Patterned sauces

An elegant sauce is the finishing touch for many special desserts. Moulded puddings offer a particular feast for the eyes when accompanied by an attractively patterned or swirled sauce.

1 Dribble a darker sauce in circles into a pale sauce. Mix the two sauces into a pattern with a wooden skewer.

2 Using a piping bag with a small nozzle, place dots of red fruit purée in circles on the pale sauce. Use a wooden skewer to join the dots with fine lines.

3 Use a piping bag with a small nozzle to pipe a thin spiral of fruit purée over the sauce. Draw lines with a wooden skewer from the centre to the edge and vice versa to create a 'sipders web'.

4 Pale and dark sauces can be poured separately onto a plate at the same time then lightly swirled together with a skewer to give a marbled effect.

Fruit as a decoration

Decorate fruit desserts with some fruit reserved from the recipe. Creams, mousses and ices also look good with fruit toppings.

1 Rinse bunches of redcurrants and dip them in caster sugar while still wet. Freeze until required.

2 Make a cut in towards the centre of thin slices of citrus fruits and place on the edge of the glass, or twist into spirals.

3 Blend sifted icing sugar with hot white wine to make an icing of coating consistency and, holding any sort of berry by its stalk, dip into the icing.

4 Crystallised fruits of different colours can be cut into strips, circles, flower shapes or crescents. Or the fruits can be diced and piped with rosettes of cream.

Brittle

Brittle can be purchased ready made. However, care must be taken of the use-by date as it will start to taste rancid if stored for too long. Brittle is made from praline, which tastes best when home-made. To make praline:

1 In a heavy based pan, melt 2 tbsps butter, sprinkle with 100g/4oz sugar and 100g/4oz chopped almonds, hazelnuts or peanuts. Stir while heating until the praline is a light brown. Remove from the heat immediately.

2 Tip the hot praline immediately onto a large piece of greased foil and allow to cool.

3 Crush the praline with the back of a spoon to break it up. Before serving the dessert, sprinkle the brittle over the top or over piped cream.

4 Creams which are not frozen or cannot be unmoulded cleanly can be poured into dessert glasses and layered with praline brittle, finishing with a layer of brittle.

A Dessert for Every Day of the Week

Delicious desserts made from
fresh fruit and dairy products –
nutritious and tempting

Popular Fruit Puddings

In either of these puddings the fruit can be varied according to season

Fruit Cocktail with Cream
top left

2 kiwi fruits	
1 mango	
250g/8oz blackberries	
250g/8oz redcurrants	
3 egg yolks	
50g/2oz icing sugar	
½ vanilla pod	
2 tbsps egg nog	
200ml/6 fl oz cream	

Preparation time: 30 minutes
Nutritional value:

Analysis per serving, approx:
• 2100kJ/500kcal
• 16g protein
• 41g fat
• 41g carbohydrate

Peel the kiwi fruits thinly, halve them lengthways and cut into slices. • Peel the mango and cut the flesh away from the stone, slicing into thin wedges. • Wash the blackberries and allow to drain. Wash the redcurrants and put a sprig aside for decoration. String the other berries. • Keep aside some blackberries, kiwi slices and a wedge of mango as well. • Beat the egg yolks with the icing sugar over a pan of simmering water until fluffy. • Split the vanilla pod, scrape out the pith and mix into the eggs with the egg nog. • Whip the cream until stiff and fold into the mixture. • Fill four sundae glasses with the fruit. • Cover the fruit with the cream, chill the dessert and top with the reserved fruit before serving.

Tutti Frutti
top right

1 large peach	
1 tbsp lemon juice	
4 tbsps sugar	
150g/5½oz raspberries	
250g/8oz ripe gooseberries	
2 eggs	
500ml/16 fl oz milk	
4 tbsps cornflour	
1 vanilla pod	
8 sponge fingers	

Preparation time: 30 minutes
Chilling time: 1 hour
Nutritional value:

Analysis per serving, approx:
• 1500kJ/360kcal
• 14g protein
• 12g fat
• 47g carbohydrate

Dip the peach briefly in boiling water, then peel it, halve the fruit and discard the stone. Now cut the halves into wedges, sprinkle with lemon juice and sprinkle with 2 tbsps sugar. • Wash the berries, clean and drain them, mix with the peach wedges, cover and set aside. • Separate the eggs. • Take 6 tbsps milk and mix well with the egg yolks and cornflour. • Split the vanilla pod, scrape out the inside and add it, the pod halves and the remaining sugar to the milk. • Bring the remainder of the milk to the boil while stirring, add the cornflour mixture and bring to the boil. Remove from the heat and discard the vanilla pod halves. • Beat the egg whites stiffly and stir into the slightly cooled custard. • Break the biscuits into pieces and fill a bowl with alternating layers of sponge fingers, fruit, and vanilla custard. Chill the dessert in the refrigerator before serving.

Fruit Blancmanges

Use peaches and strawberries in season

Vanilla Blancmange with Strawberries
top left

2 tbsps cornflour	
250ml/8 fl oz milk	
Pinch of salt	
2 tbsps sugar	
1 egg yolk	
400g/14oz strawberries	
200ml/6 fl oz whipping cream	
4 tsps vanilla sugar	

Preparation time: 40 minutes
Chilling time: 50 minutes
Nutritional value:
Analysis per serving, approx:
• 1600kJ/360kcal
• 8g protein
• 27g fat
• 26g carbohydrate

Blend the cornflour with 5 tbsps milk, then whisk in the salt, sugar and egg yolk. • Bring the remaining milk to the boil and remove from the heat. Pour the egg yolk mixture into the hot milk and return to the boil, stirring constantly. • Cool the custard over a pan of cold water and ice cubes, stirring several times to prevent a skin forming. • Wash and drain the strawberries. Reserve eight strawberries; hull and quarter the rest. • Whip the cream with the vanilla sugar until stiff and refrigerate a third of the mixture. Fold the remaining whipped cream into the cold blancmange. • Put half the blancmange into a bowl, arrange the strawberries on top and cover with the rest of the blancmange. • Decorate with the whipped cream and the reserved strawberries before serving.

Peach Ring
top right

Ingredients for one ring mould:	
3 eggs	
250ml/8 fl oz peach juice	
350ml/14 fl oz dry white wine	
2 tbsps vanilla sugar	
2 tbsps sugar	
50g/2oz cornflour	
500g/1lb 2oz yellow peaches	
Butter for the baking dish	

Preparation time: 30 minutes
Chilling time: 2 hours
Nutritional value:
Analysis per serving (serves 8):
• 780kJ/190kcal
• 5g protein
• 6g fat
• 21g carbohydrate

Separate the eggs. Beat the whites until stiff. • Heat the peach juice with the white wine, vanilla sugar and sugar. • Mix the cornflour with 4 tbsps cold water and add to the juice mixture. Bring the mixture to the boil and remove from the heat. Mix 2 tbsps of the mixture with the egg yolks and gradually beat the yolks into the thickened wine-and-juice mixture. Fold the beaten egg white into the mixture when slightly cooled. • Dip the peaches one by one in boiling water and remove the skins; then halve them and remove the stones. • Lightly butter the ring mould and line it with the peach halves, cut side uppermost • Pour the wine-and-juice mixture over the peaches and allow to set in the refrigerator. • Loosen the edges of the blancmange with a knife, dip the mould briefly in hot water and turn the Peach Ring onto a plate.

Rhubarb with Double Cream

Ideal for those who do not like their desserts too sweet

Rhubarb Dessert

A tangy fresh dessert

4 gelatine leaves or 2 tsps powdered gelatine
125ml/4 fl oz water (if using leaf gelatine)
500g/1lb 2oz rhubarb
250g/8oz strawberries
2 tbsps white wine
3 tbsps sugar
2 tsps vanilla sugar
Juice and grated rind of 1 lemon
125ml/4 fl oz double cream

Preparation time: 30 minutes
Chilling time: 45 minutes
Nutritional value:
Analysis per serving, approx:
• 890kJ/210kcal
• 4g protein
• 12g fat
• 20g carbohydrate

Soak leaf gelatine, if using, in the water. • Wash and dry the rhubarb, trim off the root ends and remove any stringy parts. • Cut the rhubarb into chunks. •

Wash the strawberries, allow to drain then hull and halve or quarter them, depending on size. • Stew the rhubarb in a covered saucepan with the wine, sugar, vanilla sugar, lemon juice and rind for 5 minutes. After 2 minutes, add the strawberries. • Remove the saucepan from the heat and allow the fruit to cool slightly. • Squeeze out the leaf gelatine and dissolve it in the warm fruit (if using powdered gelatine, follow directions on packet) • Place the rhubarb and strawberry mixture in a serving bowl or in individual dishes and leave to set in the refrigerator. • Whip the double cream and decorate the dessert with it before serving.

600g/1lb 5oz rhubarb
125ml/4 fl oz dry white wine
250ml/8 fl oz water
Juice of 1 lemon
100g/4oz sugar
50g/2oz cornflour
2 tbsps vanilla sugar
100g/4oz sponge fingers
1 tbsp sugar
Generous pinch of ground cinnamon
200ml/6 fl oz cream

Preparation time: 25 minutes
Chilling time: 1 hour
Nutritional value:
Analysis per serving, approx:
• 2200kJ/520kcal
• 8g protein
• 19g fat
• 76g carbohydrate

Trim the root ends of the rhubarb and remove any stringy bits. • Wash the rhubarb and cut into 1cm-long chunks. •

Mix the wine with the water, lemon juice and sugar, add the rhubarb and heat gently for 5 minutes with lid on. • Blend the cornflour with the vanilla sugar and 4 tbsps cold water. Mix into the rhubarb, boil up once and remove from the heat. • Rinse 4 individual dishes or one large serving dish with cold water and then pour in the dessert. Leave to cool in the refrigerator. • Place the sponge fingers between sheets of cling film and crush them with a rolling pin. • Whip the cream and fold in sugar and cinnamon. • Pipe the whipped cream over the dessert and sprinkle with the sponge finger crumbs.

Kiwi Fruit Pudding with Grenadine Cream

Kiwi fruit contains about twice as much vitamin C as oranges or lemons

6 kiwi fruits (5 very ripe)
1 grapefruit
350ml/14 fl oz dry white wine
75g/3oz sugar
40g/1½oz cornflour
½ tsp ground ginger
1 pink-fleshed grapefruit
200g/7oz crème fraîche
6 tbsps grenadine syrup

Preparation time: 40 minutes
Chilling time: 1 hour
Nutritional value:
Analysis per serving, approx:
- 2100kJ/500kcal
- 4g protein
- 20g fat
- 66g carbohydrate

Peel the 5 very ripe kiwis thinly with a knife. • Quarter them and cut into slices. • Squeeze the white grapefruit and reserve the juice. • Bring the wine and sugar to the boil. • Blend the cornflour and ginger with the grapefruit juice, add to the wine, bring to the boil again and then remove from the heat. • Mix the kiwi slices with the slightly cooled wine mixture, divide among four dessert dishes or add to a large serving bowl and place in the refrigerator. • Peel the firm kiwi fruit and slice it thinly. Carefully peel the pink grapefruit and cut into segments, removing all the pith. • Combine the crème fraîche and grenadine syrup. • Before serving, cover the kiwi pudding with the pink grapefruit segments and thin kiwi slices, and pour the grenadine cream over them.

Our Tip: For children, use apple or pineapple juice instead of wine. For a dessert that is lower in calories, replace half or all the crème fraîche with low-fat yogurt.

Buttermilk and Yogurt Desserts

Desserts rich in protein which are also good sources of vitamins

Buttermilk Jelly
top left

500g/1lb 2oz strawberries

8 leaves clear gelatine or 3¹/₂ tsps powdered gelatine

250ml/8 fl oz water (omit if using powdered gelatine)

500ml/16 fl oz buttermilk

2 tbsps lemon juice

¹/₂ tsp grated lemon rind

3 tbsps sugar

4 drops red food colouring

1 tsp oil

Preparation time: 30 minutes
Setting time: 4 hours
Nutritional value:
Analysis per serving, approx:
• 640kJ/150kcal
• 10g protein
• 3g fat
• 22g carbohydrate

Wash, hull and purée half the strawberries. • Cover and refrigerate the rest. • Soak the leaf gelatine in the water. • Mix the buttermilk with the strawberry purée, lemon juice and rind, and the sugar. • Squeeze the liquid from the gelatine and dissolve it in a small saucepan over a pan of hot water by stirring (if using powdered gelatine, follow directions on packet). • Blend the softened gelatine into one quarter of the strawberry milk then stir in the rest of the strawberry milk and the red colouring. • Oil four individual fluted moulds, pour in the jelly and leave to set in the refrigerator. • Before serving, wash and hull the remaining strawberries. • Run the tip of a knife around the edges to loosen the jelly, immerse briefly in hot water and turn out onto plates. Decorate each portion with strawberries.

Blood Orange-Yogurt Dessert
top right

9 leaves gelatine or 1 packet powdered gelatine

250ml/8 fl oz water (omit if using powdered gelatine)

600 ml/1 pint Greek-style plain yogurt

4 tbsps sugar

3 tsps vanilla sugar

4 blood oranges

250ml/8 fl oz whipping cream

1 tsp oil

2 tbsps chopped pistachios

Preparation time: 40 minutes
Setting time: 4 hours
Nutritional value:
Analysis per serving, approx:
• 1900kJ/450kcal
• 13g protein
• 30g fat
• 34g carbohydrate

Soak the leaf gelatine in the cold water, or if using powdered gelatine follow the directions on the packet. • Mix the yogurt with the sugar, vanilla sugar and juice of 2 oranges. • Squeeze the liquid from the leaf gelatine, place the gelatine (leaf or powdered) in a small bowl and soften over a pan of hot water. • Mix the gelatine into a quarter of the yogurt mixture and then blend this with the rest of the yogurt. Set aside to cool. • Whip the cream until stiff and fold into the yogurt mixture as it begins to set. • Brush four individual bowls or one large bowl with the oil, fill with the mixture and leave to set in the refrigerator. • Peel the 2 remaining oranges and divide into segments, removing all the pith. • Run the tip of a knife around the edges of the dishes. Dip the bowls briefly in hot water and turn out the jelly. Arrange the orange segments around the edge and sprinkle with pistachios.

Fruit Soup – a Refreshing Dessert

A pleasant surprise dessert

Red Berry Soup
top left

250g/8oz blackberries	
250g/8oz raspberries	
250g/8oz redcurrants	
2 tbsps cornflour	
250ml/8 fl oz blackcurrant juice	
2 tbsps sugar	

Preparation time: 30 minutes
Cooling time: 1 hour
Nutritional value:
Analysis per serving, approx:
• 660kJ/160kcal
• 3g protein
• 1g fat
• 34g carbohydrate

Wash the blackberries and raspberries several times in a bowl of cold water. • Wash the redcurrants and remove the stalks. Drain all the fruit. • Blend the cornflour with 4 tbsps of blackcurrant juice. • Mix the rest of the juice with the sugar in a saucepan, bring to the boil and add the berries. Add the cornflour and return to the boil. • Place the pudding in a bowl or in four individual bowls and leave to cool in the refrigerator. • Serve the pudding with double or clotted cream, if desired, and accompany with macaroons or brandy snaps.

Our Tip: A green gooseberry pudding also tastes good, but the gooseberries must first be cooked until soft but not yet a pulp.

Fruit Pudding with Plums
top right

750g/1lb 10oz ripe plums	
125ml/4 fl oz red wine	
125ml/4 fl oz water	
5 tbsps sugar	
½ cinnamon stick	
1 small piece of lemon rind	
2 tbsps cornflour	

Preparation time: 30 minutes
Cooling time: 1 hour
Nutritional value:
Analysis per serving, approx:
• 910kJ/220kcal
• 2g protein
• 0g fat
• 46g carbohydrate

Wash and dry the plums, quarter them and remove the stones. • Mix the red wine with the water, sugar, cinnamon and lemon rind and bring to the boil. • Add the plums to this liquid and return to the boil. • Blend 4 tbsps cold water with the cornflour. Remove the plum mixture from the heat, add the cornflour mixture and return to the boil. Remove the cinnamon stick and lemon rind. • Transfer the fruit pudding to a serving bowl or four individual bowls and, when cool, put in the refrigerator to set.

Wild Strawberry Cream on Millet

Those who like a wholefood diet will paticularly enjoy this unusual dessert

500ml/16 fl oz milk

1 tsp vanilla essence

100g/4oz raw cane sugar

150g/5¹/₂oz millet

150g/5¹/₂oz wild strawberries

1 tbsp lemon juice

¹/₂ tsp grated lemon rind

2 tsps powdered gelatine

200g/7oz quark or other low-fat curd cheese

2 eggs

125ml/4 fl oz whipping cream

Whole strawberries for decoration (optional)

Preparation time: 40 minutes
Cooking time: 50 minutes
Nutritional value:
Analysis per serving, approx:
• 2200kJ/520kcal
• 23g protein
• 21g fat
• 62g carbohydrate

Gently simmer the milk with the vanilla, 30g/1oz raw cane sugar and the millet for 20 minutes on a low heat. Cover and continue to cook, covered, for a further 30 minutes. • Hull the strawberries, wash in cold water, drain and mix with the lemon juice and rind and 20g/³/₄oz raw cane sugar, cover and leave for at least 30 minutes. • Mix the gelatine with 2 tbsps cold water and leave to stand for 10 minutes. • Allow the millet to cool down and transfer to a serving dish. • Purée the strawberries and mix with the quark. • Dissolve the softened gelatine over a very low heat, stirring constantly, and then blend with the strawberry mixture. • Beat the eggs with the remaining sugar until fluffy. • Whip the cream until stiff and fold into the strawberry mixture, together with the egg mixture. Pour this over the millet and refrigerate before serving. If desired decorate with whole strawberries.

Tempting Fruit Combinations

Delicate desserts requiring chilling time in the refrigerator

Strawberry Cream
top left

4 leaves of gelatine or 2 tsps powdered gelatine	
125ml/4 fl oz water (omit if using powdered gelatine)	
500g/1lb 2oz strawberries	
3 eggs	
½ a lemon	
100g/4oz caster sugar	
200ml/6 fl oz whipping cream	
25g/1oz plain chocolate	

Preparation time: 30 minutes
Nutritional value:
Analysis per serving, approx:
- 1900kJ/450kcal
- 14g protein
- 27g fat
- 40g carbohydrate

Soak leaf gelatine in the water. If using powdered gelatine, follow the directions on the packet• Wash and drain the strawberries and set aside 8 attractive ones for decoration. • Remove the hulls from the other strawberries and mash with a fork. •Separate the eggs. • Wash the lemon in warm water, dry it, grate the rind and squeeze out the juice. • Beat the egg yolks with the sugar over a pan of simmering water until they are fluffy and the sugar is dissolved. Squeeze the gelatine and dissolve it in the lemon juice. • Blend the gelatine into 2 tablespoons of strawberry mixture, then add the rest of the mixture. • Leave the strawberry cream in the refrigerator to chill. •Whip the cream and the egg whites separately until both are stiff. • Place half the whipped cream in the refrigerator. Stir the remaining cream and the beaten egg white into the strawberry cream. • Transfer the strawberry cream to a glass bowl and decorate with the reserved strawberries, the whipped cream and the grated chocolate. • Chill the dessert before serving.

Yogurt Ring with Nectarines
top right

Ingredients for 1 ring-shaped mould:	
9 leaves gelatine or 1 packet powdered gelatine	
250ml/8 fl oz water (omit if using powdered gelatine)	
1 lemon	
1 vanilla pod	
4 tbsps sugar	
1kg/2¼lbs yogurt	
250ml/8 fl oz cream	
5 nectarines	
2 tbsps sugar	
1 tbsp orange liqueur	
50g/2oz chopped pistachios	

Preparation time: 45 minutes
Setting time: 4 hours
Nutritional value:
Analysis per serving (serves 8):
- 1260kJ/300kcal
- 9g protein
- 19g fat
- 23g carbohydrate

Soak the leaf gelatine in the water. • Grate the lemon rind and extract the juice. • Split the vanilla pod, scrape out the inside and stir into the yogurt with the 4 tbsps sugar, lemon rind and juice. • Squeeze the water out of the gelatine. Heat 3 tbsps water, add the squeezed gelatine or, if using powdered gelatine, follow directions on packet. Slowly add the yogurt mixture and mix well. • Whip the cream until stiff and mix in. • Rinse the mould with cold water, pour in the yogurt mixture and leave to set in the refrigerator. • Scald the nectarines with boiling water, remove the skin, halve them, remove the stones and cut into pieces. • Mix the nectarines with the 2 tbsps sugar, the liqueur and the pistachios and chill in the refrigerator. • Unmould the yogurt ring onto a plate and fill the centre with nectarines.

Berry Pot-Pourri

Rich in protein and vitamins if served with cottage cheese

Currant Cream

Made with red- and blackcurrants

| 250g/8oz strawberries, hulled |
| 200g/7oz redcurrants |
| 125g/5oz bilberries |
| 125g/5oz raspberries |
| 5 tbsps sugar |
| 1/2 vanilla pod |
| 1 lemon |
| 125ml/4 fl oz whipping cream |
| 500g/1lb 2oz cottage cheese |

Preparation time: 30 minutes
Marinating time: 6 hours
Nutritional value:
Analysis per serving, approx:
• 1500kJ/360kcal
• 20g protein
• 16g fat
• 31g carbohydrate

Wash the strawberries and redcurrants, dry and remove the stalks. • Rinse the bilberries and raspberries several times in a bowl of water, and drain thoroughly. • Mix all the fruit with 4 tbsps sugar, cover and leave to marinate for 6 hours in the refrigerator. • Split the vanilla pod and scrape out the inside. • Wash the lemon in hot water, dry and finely grate the rind. • Whip the cream with the vanilla and the remainder of the sugar until stiff and stir in the grated lemon rind. • Break down the cheese with a fork and fold in the whipped cream. Arrange the dessert in a bowl or on individual plates; top with the chilled fruit.

| 250g/8oz each of red and blackcurrants, washed and drained |
| 6 leaves of gelatine or 2 1/2 tsps powdered gelatine |
| 250ml/8 fl oz water (omit if using powdered gelatine) |
| 3 eggs |
| 125ml/4 fl oz milk |
| 2 tbsps vanilla sugar |
| 100g/4oz sugar |
| 200ml/6 fl oz whipping cream |
| 2 tbsps egg liqueur |

Preparation time: 30 minutes
Chilling time: 1 hour
Nutritional value:
Analysis per serving, approx:
• 2100kJ/500kcal
• 16g protein
• 26g fat
• 47g carbohydrate

Reserve a few of the fruits for decoration, purée the remainder in a liquidiser and then push the mixture through a fine sieve• Soak the leaf gelatine in the water. • Separate the eggs. • Boil the milk. • Beat the egg yolks with the vanilla sugar and 75g/3oz sugar over a pan of simmering water until fluffy. Add the hot milk in a steady stream, and continue to beat constantly, over a pan of hot water, for 5 minutes. Remove from the heat. • Squeeze out the gelatine and dissolve in the hot milk mixture (if using powdered, follow directions on packet). • Mix the gelatine into the fruit purée gradually and leave to set in the refrigerator. • Whisk the egg whites until stiff. • Whip the cream and the remaining sugar until it forms soft peaks. Fold half the whipped cream and the beaten egg whites into the fruit cream when it starts to set. Transfer the mixture to four glass dessert bowls and return to the refrigerator. • Mix the remaining whipped cream with the egg liqueur and pour this over the dessert just before serving. Sprinkle with the reserved sprigs of redcurrants or blackcurrants.

Innovative Ways with Strawberries

Perfect desserts for the height of the strawberry season

Strawberry Mousse
top left

4 leaves of gelatine or 2 tsps powdered gelatine	
125ml/4 fl oz water (omit if using powdered gelatine)	
400g/14oz strawberries	
125ml/4 fl oz milk	
Generous pinch of cinnamon	
2 eggs	
50g/2oz sugar	
1 tsp lemon juice	
200ml/6 fl oz whipping cream	
2 tbsps chopped almonds	

Preparation time: 40 minutes
Chilling time: 3 hours
Nutritional value:
Analysis per serving, approx:
• 1600kJ/380kcal
• 12g protein
• 26g fat
• 24g carbohydrate

Soak the gelatine leaves in the water. •Reserve 12 strawberries for decoration and leave, covered, in the refrigerator. • Wash, drain and hull the remaining strawberries. Push the strawberries through a fine sieve. • Boil up the milk with the cinnamon then remove from the heat. • Separate the eggs. • Beat the egg yolks with the sugar until fluffy and add the hot milk in a thin stream. • Squeeze the water from the leaf gelatine and stir it into the warm liquid to dissolve it (if using powdered, follow directions on packet). • Beat the egg-and-milk mixture to a creamy consistency. • Whisk the egg whites with the lemon juice into stiff peaks. • Whip the cream until stiff, then chill one third of it in the refrigerator. Blend the strawberry purée with the egg mixture and fold in the remaining cream. Lastly, add the beaten egg white. • Transfer the mousse to a bowl and leave to set in the refrigerator.

• Before serving, decorate with the reserved cream, strawberries and chopped almonds.

Strawberry Cup
top right

400ml/15 fl oz milk	
4 tbsps sugar	
100g/4oz short-grain rice	
500g/1lb 2oz strawberries	
200ml/6 fl oz whipping cream	
3 tsps vanilla sugar	
Grated rind of 1 lemon	

Preparation time: 1 hour
Chilling time: 1 hour
Nutritional value:
Analysis per serving, approx:
• 1700kJ/400kcal
• 8g protein
• 21g fat
• 49g carbohydrate

Bring the milk to the boil with 1 tbsp sugar. Sprinkle the rice into the milk and cook for 40 minutes on a very low heat in an uncovered saucepan. Stir several times, as rice pudding burns easily. • Meanwhile, wash and drain the strawberries, hull, quarter and sprinkle with the remaining sugar. Cover and leave in the refrigerator. • Place the cooked rice pudding over a pan of cold water containing ice cubes and stir frequently to cool it rapidly. Leave the cold rice in the refrigerator for 30 minutes. • Whip the cream with the vanilla sugar until stiff. • Divide the rice pudding between four glass dessert bowls, arrange the strawberries on top and cover with whipped cream. Sprinkle each portion with a little grated lemon rind.

Fruit Jelly with Vanilla Cream

An unusual peach and apricot dessert

4 leaves of gelatine or 2 tsps powdered gelatine
125ml/4 fl oz water (omit if using powdered gelatine)
½ vanilla pod
125ml/4 fl oz milk
300g/10oz mixed ripe berries
1 peach
2 apricots
7 tbsps sugar
250ml/8 fl oz medium-sweet white wine
2 egg yolks
3 tbsps sugar

Preparation time: 45 minutes
Chilling time: 4 hours
Nutritional value:

Analysis per serving, approx:
• 1500kJ/360kcal
• 12g protein
• 18g fat
• 35g carbohydrate

Soak the gelatine leaves in the water. • Split the vanilla pod and scrape out the inside. Add the leaf gelatine, if using, and the vanilla pulp to the milk and bring to the boil; remove from the heat. • Wash the berries and leave to drain. • Peel, halve and stone the peach. • Wash, dry, halve and stone the apricots and dice them with the peaches. • Mix the diced fruit and berries with 4 tbsps of the sugar. • Warm up the white wine. Press the liquid from the gelatine and dissolve the liquid in the wine (if using powdered, follow directions on packet). • Place some fruit at the bottom of a bowl, pour a little of the gelatine mixture over it and leave to set in the refrigerator. • Mix the rest of the gelatine with the fruit, pour this over the set jelly and then return to the refrigerator. • Remove the vanilla from the milk and bring back to the boil. • Whisk the egg yolks with the remainder of the sugar until fluffy. Trickle the hot milk slowly into the yolks and sugar, and stir over a gentle heat until the mixture thickens, but do not allow it to boil. Chill the vanilla cream. • Unmould the jelly onto a plate and serve with the vanilla cream.

Red Cherries with Black Bread

An unconventional combination for the diet-conscious

150g/5½oz stale rye wholemeal bread, crusts removed
2 tbsps clear honey
1 tbsp Maraschino or cherry brandy
½ tsp ground cinnamon
400g/14oz red cherries
1 tbsp raw cane sugar
200ml/6 fl oz whipping cream

Preparation time: 30 minutes
Nutritional value:
Analysis per serving, approx:
• 1400kJ/330kcal
• 5g protein
• 17g fat
• 39g carbohydrate

Cut the bread into slices and crumble it (if it is too stale to do this, crush it with a rolling pin under cling film). • Mix the breadcrumbs with half the honey, the Maraschino and the cinnamon. • Wash, dry and stone the cherries, and mix with the raw cane sugar. • Whip the cream with the rest of the honey until stiff. • Fill four glass dessert bowls with alternate layers of the bread mixture, cherries, and the honey cream, finishing with a layer of cream. Crumble some reserved breadcrumbs onto each portion.

Our Tip: If the dessert is made with sweet cherries, the sugar may be omitted. This dessert tastes particularly delicious when 50g/2oz finely-chopped hazelnuts are added to the bread mixture and chopped nuts are sprinkled over the top layer of cream.

Imaginative Desserts

Old favourites - but with a new twist

Plums and Custard
top left

FOR THE PLUMS:

500g/1lb 2oz plums	
¹/₂ a lemon	
¹/₂ cinnamon stick	
2 cloves	
2 tbsps sugar	
125ml/4 fl oz dry red wine	

FOR THE CUSTARD:

1 vanilla pod	
125ml/4 fl oz milk	
5 egg yolks	
4 tbsps sugar	
250ml/8 fl oz double cream	

Preparation time: 1¹/₄ hours
Nutritional value:
Analysis per serving, approx:
• 1930kJ/460kcal
• 23g protein
• 61g fat
• 35g carbohydrate

Wash and dry the plums, cut them in half and stone them. • Wash the lemon in warm water, dry it, cut off a piece of rind and squeeze out the juice. • Put the plums in a saucepan, add the cinnamon stick, lemon rind and juice, cloves, sugar and red wine, and bring to the boil, covered. Simmer for 10 minutes. • Pour the compote into a bowl and leave it to cool. • To make the custard, split the vanilla pod lengthways. • Bring the milk to the boil with the vanilla pod, then remove from the heat; cover and leave to infuse for 10 minutes. • Beat the egg yolks with the sugar over a pan of simmering water until pale and fluffy. • Remove the vanilla pod from the milk. • Stir the cream and the warm milk into the egg yolk mixture and beat this over a pan of hot water until it thickens. Leave the mixture to cool, stirring frequently to prevent a skin forming. Pour the custard over the compote before serving.

Pink Cloudlets
top right

7 leaves gelatine or 1 packet powdered gelatine	
250ml/8 fl oz water (omit if using powdered gelatine)	
250g/8oz strawberries	
75g/3oz sugar	
2 tbsps vanilla sugar	
500ml/16 fl oz whipping cream	
150g/5¹/₂oz natural yogurt	
1 lemon	
2 tbsps icing sugar	

Preparation time: 20 minutes
Setting time: 1 hour
Nutritional value:
Analysis per serving, approx:
• 2400kJ/570kcal
• 8g protein
• 41g fat
• 41g carbohydrate

Soak the leaf gelatine in the cold water. • Wash, drain and hull the strawberries. Reserve a few of the strawberries for decoration. • Sprinkle the sugar and vanilla sugar over the other strawberries and mash with a fork. • Beat half the cream with the yogurt until fluffy. • Wash the lemon in warm water and dry it. Grate the rind and squeeze out the juice. • Squeeze out the leaf gelatine. Heat the lemon juice and dissolve the gelatine in it (if using powdered gelatine, follow directions on the packet). Mix the dissolved gelatine with 3 tbsps of yogurt mixture, then add the rind and the rest of the mixture. • Chill until it begins to thicken. • Whip the remaining cream until stiff, combine with the strawberry purée and blend into the yogurt mixture. Leave to set in the refrigerator. • Sift the icing sugar over four dessert plates. Wet a tablespoon and spoon the mixture onto the plates. Decorate the pink cloudlets with the reserved

Caramel Apples with Calvados

Orange-flavoured liqueur may be used instead of Calvados

Cold Melon Soup

A refreshing snack on hot days

4 cooking apples
2 tsps lemon juice
150g/5¹/₂oz sugar
1 clove
175ml/5 fl oz still mineral water
200ml/7 fl oz Calvados

Preparation time: 40 minutes
Marinating time: 1 hour
Nutritional value:
Analysis per serving, approx:
• 980kJ/230kcal•
• 1g protein
• 1g fat
• 54g carbohydrate

Peel and quarter the apples. Remove the cores, slice the quarters and sprinkle with lemon juice. • Reserve 3 tbsps of the mineral water in a separate pan. Heat up 100g/4oz of the sugar with the clove and the rest of the mineral water in a saucepan, stirring until the sugar is completely dissolved. • Add the slices of apple to the syrup, cover and simmer over a gentle heat for 15 minutes. Transfer the apple mixture to a shallow bowl. • Remove the clove and boil the syrup, uncovered, until it thickens. Remove from the heat, add the Calvados and pour this over the apple segments. • Allow the apples to cool, then cover and leave in the refrigerator to marinate. • Melt the remaining sugar with the reserved mineral water in a pan over a low heat; bring to the boil stirring constantly and continue stirring until the sugar has caramelised to a light brown. • Drizzle the caramel in thin threads over the apple.

2 leaves gelatine or 1 tsp powdered gelatine
125ml/4 fl oz water (omit if using powdered gelatine)
1 charentais and 1 honeydew melon each weighing 750g/1lb 10oz
2 oranges
100g/4oz raw cane sugar
1 lemon
2 tbsps orange liqueur
1 sprig of lemon balm (optional)
Ice cubes

Preparation time: 20 minutes
Chilling time: 1 hour
Nutritional value:
Analysis per serving, approx:
• 990kJ/240kcal
• 5g protein
• 0g fat
• 52g carbohydrate

Soak the leaf gelatine in the cold water. • Quarter the melons and remove the seeds. Scoop out the flesh from one quarter of each melon using a melon baller. • Peel the remaining quarters and cut the flesh into small cubes. • Squeeze the juice from the oranges, add with the sugar to the melon quarters, and purée the mixture. • Wash the lemon in warm water, dry and peel thinly. Cut the rind into very fine julienne strips. • Squeeze the lemon juice and heat it. • Squeeze out the gelatine and add it to the lemon juice or dissolve the powdered gelatine in the hot lemon juice. Add with the orange liqueur to the fruit purée. • Add the melon balls to the cold soup and chill before serving. • Rinse the lemon balm in lukewarm water, wipe it dry, pull off leaves and sprinkle them over the soup with the crushed ice cubes.

Seasonal Fruit Desserts

Use only fresh fruit for these dishes

Blackberry Cream
top left

| 4 leaves red gelatine or 1 packet red jelly |
| 250ml/8 fl oz water |
| 500g/1lb 2oz blackberries |
| 100g/4oz raw cane sugar |
| 8 tbsps apple juice |
| 1 apple |
| 2 tsps lemon juice |
| 125ml/4 fl oz whipping cream |
| 2 egg whites |
| Pinch of salt |

Preparation time: 30 minutes
Chilling time: 1 hour
Nutritional value:
Analysis per serving, approx:
• 1300kJ/310kcal
• 9g protein
• 13g fat
• 42g carbohydrate

Soak the leaf gelatine, if using, in the cold water or, if using packet jelly, make it up with water according to the packet directions. • Wash the blackberries and drain in a sieve. Reserve 20 attractive berries. • Bring the remaining blackberries to the boil with the sugar and apple juice, cover, and cook for 10 minutes over a low heat. Pass through a fine sieve, then reheat but do not allow to boil. • Squeeze the leaf gelatine and dissolve in the purée. If using packet jelly, mix it with the purée before the jelly has set. Refrigerate the jelly mixture. • Wash, dry and grate the apple. Mix the grated apple with the lemon juice and add to the purée. • Whip the cream until stiff. Whisk the egg whites with the salt until stiff. • When the fruit jelly begins to set, fold in the whipped cream and egg whites and chill in the refrigerator. • Decorate the dessert with the reserved blackberries.

Figs in Port Wine
top right

| 500g/1lb 2oz fresh figs |
| 2 tbsps honey |
| 3 tbsps lemon juice |
| 125ml/4 fl oz port wine |
| 200ml/6 fl oz cream |
| 1 banana |

Preparation time: 30 minutes
Chilling time: 30 minutes
Nutritional value:
Analysis per serving, approx:
• 1500kJ/360kcal
• 4g protein
• 16g fat
• 42g carbohydrate

Wash and dry the figs and remove the stalks. • Starting from the stalk end, peel off the skin bit by bit with a knife. Cut the figs into slices and arrange them on a plate. • Gently heat the honey with the lemon juice, stirring all the time, until the honey and juice are well mixed. • Pour the port over the figs, add the lemon and honey and leave, covered, in the refrigerator for 30 minutes. • Whip the cream until nearly stiff. • Peel the banana, reserve a few slices, dice the rest and purée in the liquidiser or food processor. Combine with the cream. • Pour the cream over the figs and carefully mix in with two forks. Decorate the dessert with the banana slices.

Our Tip: To adapt this dessert for children, marinate the figs in freshly squeezed orange juice instead of port. The banana cream can be sweetened with 2 tbsps hazelnut spread (available from healthfood shops).

Popular Fruit Desserts

Quinces and nuts are in season at the same time

Filled Orange Halves
top left

4 oranges	
50g/2oz shelled walnuts	
1 banana	
100g/4oz chocolate sweetened with cane sugar	
250ml/8 fl oz whipping cream	
1 tbsp cocoa powder	
1 tbsp orange blossom honey	

Preparation time: 50 minutes
Nutritional value:
Analysis per serving, approx:
- 2200kJ/520kcal
- 7g protein
- 36g fat
- 46g carbohydrate

Wash the oranges in warm water, dry them and cut in half crossways. Use a sharp-edged teaspoon to scoop out the flesh; place it in a sieve to drain. •

Remove the pips from the fruit. • Remove the skin from the orange halves and cut a thin sliver of peel from the round end of each orange half so that they will sit flat. • Place two halves on each dessert plate. • Chop the walnuts coarsely and roast in a dry pan, turning them until they darken and smell good. • Peel the banana, cut in half lengthways and slice. • Break the chocolate into pieces, melt with 100ml/3 fl oz cream in a bowl over a pan of simmering water on a low heat and stir in the cocoa powder. • Leave half the mixture over the pan of hot water. • Mix the rest of the chocolate with the banana slices, nuts, honey and orange pulp. • Whip the rest of the cream until stiff, fold into the orange mixture, divide among the orange halves and sprinkle with the remaining chocolate.

Quince Foam
top right

2 leaves gelatine or 1 tsp powdered gelatine	
125ml/4 fl oz water (omit if using powdered gelatine)	
300g/10oz quinces	
300g/10oz cooking apples	
1/2 vanilla pod	
1 cinnamon stick	
1/4 tsp coriander seeds	
300ml/14 fl oz water	
70g/3oz orange blossom honey	
200ml/6 fl oz whipping cream	
2 tbsps orange liqueur	
40g/1 1/2oz shelled walnuts	

Preparation time: 50 minutes
Chilling time: 1 hour
Nutritional value:
Analysis per serving, approx:
- 1600kJ/380kcal
- 4g protein
- 23g fat
- 38g carbohydrate

Soak the leaf gelatine in the cold water. • Wash the quinces and apples thoroughly in lukewarm water and chop coarsely, leaving the peel on. • Split the vanilla pod and scrape out the inside. Place both with the fruit, the cinnamon stick, the coriander and the water in a covered saucepan over a medium heat and cook for at least 20 minutes. • Remove the vanilla pod and cinnamon. • Pass the fruit through a fine sieve. • Squeeze the gelatine and add it to the fruit purée or add the teaspoon of powdered gelatine to the purée. Mix the honey into the purée and leave to cool. • Whip the cream until stiff and mix with the orange liqueur. • Chop the walnuts. • Stir two-thirds of the whipped cream into the fruit purée and place in four dessert glasses or a serving bowl and refrigerate. • Decorate with the remaining whipped cream and sprinkle with the chopped nuts before serving.

Rich Raspberry Cream

A mouthwatering Italian dessert

500g/1lb 2oz raspberries
4 tbsps icing sugar
3 tbsps grappa or raspberry liqueur
2 eggs
250g/8oz mascarpone or full-fat cream cheese
100ml/3 fl oz single cream
2 sponge fingers

Preparation time: 30 minutes
Chilling time: 2 hours
Nutritional value:

Analysis per serving, approx:
- 1800kJ/430kcal
- 11g protein
- 29g fat
- 26g carbohydrate

Rinse the raspberries several times in a bowl of water. • Drain and carefully mix with 2 tbsps of sifted icing sugar and the grappa. • Separate the eggs. Beat the yolks with the remaining icing sugar until fluffy. • Gradually add the mascarpone to the egg yolks and continue beating until a thick cream is formed. • Whisk the egg whites until stiff; whip the cream until stiff and fold both into the mascarpone cream. • Alternate layers of the cream with the raspberries in four dessert glasses, finishing with a layer of the cream mixture.

Refrigerate. • Wrap the sponge fingers in cling film and crush with a rolling pin. Sprinkle the crumbs over the dessert before serving.

Vanilla Cream with Cherries

If this is too sweet, use plain, Greek-style yogurt instead of cream

250ml/8 fl oz milk
1/2 packet instant vanilla pudding powder
1 tbsp sugar
5 tbsps milk
400g/14oz black cherries
200ml/6 fl oz whipping cream
1 tbsp vanilla sugar
2 tbsps kirsch

Preparation time: 40 minutes
Chilling time: 30 minutes
Nutritional value:

Analysis per serving, approx:
- 1400kJ/330kcal
- 5g protein
- 19g fat
- 33g carbohydrate

Bring the milk to the boil. Blend the pudding powder and sugar with 5 tbsps milk. • Remove the hot milk from the heat and stir in the pudding powder mixture. • Bring the milk back to the boil. • Place the pudding over a pan of cold water with ice cubes and stir frequently to prevent a skin forming while the pudding quickly cools. • Wash, pat dry and stone the cherries. • Whip the cream with the vanilla sugar until stiff. Place a third of the whipped cream into a piping bag with a star nozzle and place in the refrigerator. • Fold the rest of the whipped cream into the pudding with the kirsch; chill the mixture. Shortly before serving, put half the pudding into a serving dish or four individual glass bowls, arrange the cherries on top and finish with a layer of pudding. • Decorate the dessert with rosettes of cream.

Our Tip: For children, omit the kirsch. Chopped sunflower seeds may be sprinkled on the cream rosettes if desired.

Stuffed Pineapple with Yogurt Sauce

A very special Sunday dessert

| 1 medium-sized ripe pineapple |
| 2 bananas |
| 3 kiwi fruits |
| 1 ripe papaya (pawpaw) |
| 2 tbsps vanilla sugar |
| Juice of 1 lemon |
| 125ml/4 fl oz whipping cream |
| 500g/1lb 2oz yogurt |
| 1 tbsp sugar |
| 1/2 tsp ground ginger |
| 1 tsp finely chopped lemon balm |

Preparation time: 40 minutes
Chilling time: 1 hour
Nutritional value:
Analysis per serving, approx:
• 2500kJ/600kcal
• 10g protein
• 16g fat
• 100g carbohydrate

Wash the pineapple in lukewarm water and dry it. Cut a lid about 3 cm/1¼ inches in height lengthways from the pineapple. Cut a thin sliver from the other side of the pineapple so that the stuffed fruit will sit level. • Scoop out the flesh from the lid and the rest of the pineapple, making sure you do not pierce the skin. Cut the flesh into chunks and discard the central, woody core. • Peel the bananas and cut into slices. • Peel the kiwis, quarter and cut into slices. Peel the papaya, cut in half, remove its black seeds and dice the fruit. • Mix all the fruit with the vanilla sugar and lemon juice, fill the pineapple, wrap in foil and leave in the refrigerator. • Whip the cream until stiff. • Stir the sugar, ginger and lemon balm into the yogurt, fold in the whipped cream and arrange the yogurt sauce on a dish. • Place the lid of the pineapple over the fruit salad and serve the sauce with it.

Floating Islands

These attractive desserts are known in France as "oeufs à la neige"

Chocolate Floating Islands
top left

4 eggs	
3 tbsps caster sugar	
750ml/24 fl oz milk	
150g/5½oz coffee-flavoured or bitter chocolate	
1 tsp instant coffee powder	
2 tbsps cocoa powder	

Preparation time: 40 minutes
Nutritional value:
Analysis per serving, approx:
- 2100kJ/500kcal
- 21g protein
- 30g fat
- 38g carbohydrate

Separate the eggs. Whisk the egg whites until stiff and gradually add 1 tbsp sugar, continuing to beat. • Heat the milk in a shallow saucepan. • Use 2 teaspoons to scoop up lumps of egg white and place them gently in the hot milk to cook for one minute on each side over a low heat. Remove the egg whites from the milk with a slotted spoon and reserve them. • Beat the egg yolks with the rest of the sugar over a pan of simmering water until fluffy. • Break the chocolate into pieces and melt it in the hot milk. • Blend the coffee powder and cocoa with several tbsps milk and mix into the egg yolks. • Trickle the hot chocolate milk slowly into the yolk mixture, stirring, and whisk this for several more minutes over the pan of simmering water. • Place the chocolate cream in four shallow dessert bowls, float the "islands" on top and sift some cocoa powder over them.

Oeufs à la Neige
top right

1 vanilla pod	
500ml/16 fl oz milk	
4 eggs	
Pinch of salt	
160g/6½oz caster sugar	

Preparation time: 40 minutes
Chilling time: 1 to 2 hours
Nutritional value:
Analysis per serving, approx:
- 1800kJ/430kcal
- 17g protein
- 16g fat
- 52g carbohydrate

Split the vanilla pod, scrape out the inside and add both to the milk. • Separate the eggs. • Whisk the egg whites with the salt until stiff. Continue to whisk while slowly adding 50g/2oz sugar until white and glossy. • Beat the egg yolks with 50g/2oz sugar until fluffy. • Heat the milk and vanilla in a shallow pan, stirring until almost boiling. • Using two spoons remove 5 lumps of egg white, place in the gently simmering milk and cook for about one minute on each side. With a slotted spoon, transfer to a plate to drain. Continue until all the egg white has been used. • Strain the vanilla milk through a fine sieve into the egg yolk mixture and heat this mixture, stirring all the time, until almost boiling. Then remove from the heat and place the pan in a bowl with ice cubes to cool down, stir the mixture frequently to prevent a skin forming. • Transfer the custard to a glass dish. • Chill the custard and the 'snowballs' separately in the refrigerator. • Make a caramel with the remaining 3 tbsps sugar and 1 tbsp water, over a low heat. • Just before serving put the snowballs on the custard and drizzle with the caramel.

Desserts with Quark and Fruit

Both desserts can also be prepared using curd cheese

Semolina Blancmange with Bilberries
top left

500ml/16 fl oz milk	
7 tbsps sugar	
65g/2½oz semolina	
1 egg	
125g/5oz quark or low fat curd cheese	
2 tbsps lemon juice	
1 tsp grated lemon rind	
Pinch of salt	
250g/8oz bilberries	

Preparation time: 30 minutes
Chilling time: 2 hours
Nutritional value:
Analysis per serving, approx:
• 1400kJ/330kcal
• 13g protein
• 11g fat
• 45g carbohydrate

Bring the milk and 5 tbsps sugar to the boil. Gradually stir in the semolina, bring to the boil and then simmer for 5 minutes on a very low heat. • Separate the egg. • Mix the cheese with the egg yolk, 1 tbsp lemon juice and the rind and combine with the warm semolina mixture. • Set aside to cool. Whisk the egg white and salt until stiff and fold into the cooling semolina. • Rinse four dessert bowls in cold water and transfer the mixture to them. Leave to set in the refrigerator. • Wash the bilberries in a bowl of water. Drain the berries and mix them with the rest of the lemon juice and the sugar. Chill in the refrigerator. • Unmould the individual blancmanges onto plates and surround each with bilberries.

Our Tip: If bilberries are unavailable substitute blueberries.

Fruit Quark
top right

4 tbsps lemon juice	
4 tbsps clear honey	
1 apple	
1 orange	
1 banana	
400g/14oz quark or low fat curd cheese	
5 tbsps milk	
4 tsps vanilla sugar	
1 tbsp shelled hazelnuts	
1 tbsp sunflower seeds	

Preparation time: 30 minutes
Nutritional value:
Analysis per serving, approx:
• 1300kJ/310kcal
• 10g protein
• 11g fat
• 39g carbohydrate

Mix 2 tbsps lemon juice and 2 tbsps honey in a bowl. • Peel the apple, orange and banana. • Quarter, core and dice the apple. • Separate the orange into segments, quarter each segment, removing the pips, and saving any juice. • Halve the banana lengthways and slice it. • Mix the fruit with the lemon and honey mixture. • Mix the cheese with the milk, vanilla sugar, orange juice, the remaining lemon juice and the honey until creamy and add three-quarters of the fruit. • Distribute this mixture between four dessert bowls and arrange the remaining fruit on top. • Slice the hazelnuts thinly and toast in a dry pan with the sunflower seeds, stirring until golden. Allow to cool slightly and sprinkle them over the fruit.

Bilberry Cream

Quickly prepared with an electric mixer

400g/14oz bilberries	
4 tbsps sugar	
1 tsp lemon juice	
500ml/16 fl oz clotted cream	
3 tsps vanilla sugar	

Preparation time: 20 minutes
Nutritional value:

Analysis per serving, approx:
• 1300kJ/310kcal
• 6g protein
• 20g fat
• 31g carbohydrate

Rinse the bilberries several times in a bowl of water. Discard any shrivelled berries. • Leave to drain in a colander. • Mix two-thirds of the berries with 2 tbsps sugar. Reserve in the refrigerator until ready to use. • Pass the remaining bilberries through a fine sieve. • Mix the fruit purée with the lemon juice. • Set aside about 1 tbsp of the sugared bilberries. Divide the remaining bilberries between four dessert plates. • Shortly before serving, beat the clotted cream in a chilled bowl for 30 seconds until fluffy, using an electric beater on a low setting. Add the remaining sugar, vanilla sugar and fruit purée and gradually beat into the cream, continuing to beat on the top setting until the desired consistency is reached. Put cream into a piping bag with a star nozzle and pipe rosettes of the bilberry cream over the berries. Decorate each portion with the remaining berries.

Our Tip: If bilberries are unavialable substitute blueberries.

Peasant Girl in a Veil

A national dessert in Scandinavia

500g/1lb 2oz apples	
125ml/4 fl oz water	
6 tbsps sugar	
1 tbsp lemon juice	
2 tbsps butter	
8 tbsps whole oat flakes	
Generous pinch of ground cinnamon	
250ml/8 fl oz whipped cream	
4 tsps redcurrant jelly	

Preparation time: 40 minutes
Chilling time: 1 hour
Nutritional value:

Analysis per serving, approx:
• 1900kJ/450kcal
• 7g protein
• 26g fat
• 47g carbohydrate

Wash, dry, quarter and core the apples. Put in a pan with the water, cover and stew over a low heat until soft. • Purée in a liquidiser or food processor or push through a sieve. Mix the purée with 4 tbsps sugar and the lemon juice, cover and allow to cool. • Melt the butter in a pan and caramelise the remaining sugar and oats in it, stirring constantly, until it resembles crunchy oat breakfast cereal. Stir in the cinnamon, tip the mixture onto a plate and leave to cool. • Whip the cream until stiff. • Arrange alternating layers of apple mousse, cream and oats in a serving bowl or four individual bowls. Top with a layer of oats. • Decorate the dessert with blobs of whipped cream and redcurrant jelly.

Our Tip: Instead of the oats you can caramelise stale, grated wholemeal bread with the butter and sugar. For a less fattening dessert, replace the cream with crème fraîche.

Chocolate Shape

So much better when completely home-made

50g/2oz ground rice	
1 heaped tbsp cocoa powder	
Generous pinch cinnamon	
1 tsp vanilla essence	
1 tsp grated orange peel	
350ml/14 fl oz milk	
1 large banana	
50g/2oz blanched almonds	
80g/3oz honey	
2 eggs	

Preparation time: 20 minutes
Chilling time: 1 hour
Nutritional value:
Analysis per serving, approx:
• 1500kJ/360kcal
• 13g protein
• 15g fat
• 44g carbohydrate

Mix the ground rice with the cocoa, cinnamon, vanilla and orange peel and add 100ml/3 fl oz cold milk; blend until smooth. • Peel the banana, cut it in half lengthways and slice. • Grind the almonds and heat them in a small saucepan with the honey. • Stir in the rest of the milk and bring to the boil. • Blend the ground rice mixture with the hot milk and cook for a further 5 minutes over a gentle heat, stirring constantly. • Stir in the banana slices and remove the saucepan from the heat. • Separate the eggs. Remove 2 tbsps of the hot mixture and whisk it into the egg yolks, then gradually add the egg yolk mixture to the pan. Leave to cool slightly. • Whisk the egg whites until they form stiff peaks and fold them into the custard. • Rinse a bowl or ring mould with cold water and add the custard. Leave to set in the refrigerator. Shortly before serving, unmould the blancmange onto a serving plate.

Our Tip: Decorate the blancmange with blobs of cream or slivered almonds.

Cherry Cream Pudding

It is worth waiting for the black cherry season to make this delightful dessert

Ingredients for 6 portions:

1kg/2¼lbs black cherries
100g/4oz sugar
500ml/16 fl oz red wine
½ cinnamon stick
1 lemon
2 tbsps cornflour
250g/8oz cream cheese
200ml/6 fl oz sour cream
1 tbsp vanilla sugar

Preparation time: 40 minutes
Chilling time: 1 hour
Nutritional value:
Analysis per serving, approx:
- 1900kJ/450kcal
- 18g protein
- 17g fat • 50g carbohydrate

Wash, pat dry and stone the cherries. Place them in a saucepan together with the sugar, red wine and the cinnamon stick.
• Wash the lemon in warm water, dry, grate the rind and add to the cherries. • Cover the cherries and heat gently for 5 minutes. • Squeeze the lemon, stir the cornflour into the lemon juice, mix into the cherries and bring to the boil briefly. • Remove the cinnamon stick and leave to cool.
• Mix the cream cheese, the sour cream and vanilla sugar until smooth. Pour this over the fruit mixture – which should not yet have set – and gently stir in with a fork. • Rinse a glass bowl in cold water and pour the mixture into it.
• Refrigerate before serving.

Our Tip: Less calorific but not quite so tempting if 200g/7oz natural yogurt is used instead of the cream cheese and sour cream.

Famous Name Desserts

Two deliciously memorable desserts

Guelph Dessert
top left

FOR THE BLANCMANGE:

4 tbsps cornflour
500ml/16 fl oz milk
1 vanilla pod
4 tbsps sugar
3 egg whites
Pinch of salt

FOR THE SAUCE:

3 egg yolks
5 tbsps sugar
1 tbsp cornflour
250ml/8 fl oz white wine
1 tbsp lemon juice

Preparation time: 1 hour
Chilling time: 2 hours
Nutritional value:
Analysis per serving, approx:
• 1600kJ/380kcal
• 14g protein
• 13g fat
• 44g carbohydrate

Blend the cornflour with 6 tbsps milk. • Split the vanilla pod and scrape out the inside. Bring the remaining milk to the boil with the vanilla and sugar. • Add the cornflour to the milk, stir well and return to the boil. Remove from the heat and discard the vanilla pod. • Whisk the egg whites with the salt until stiff and fold into the blancmange. • Divide the blancmange between four dessert bowls and refrigerate. • Combine the yolks with the sugar, cornflour, white wine and lemon juice and heat gently, whisking until the liquid foams. • Remove from the heat and continue beating for 2 minutes to cool it quickly. • Pour the sauce over the blancmange and chill.

Diplomat Pudding
top right

Ingredients for 8 people:

4 leaves gelatine or 2 tsps powdered gelatine
125ml/4 fl oz water (omit if using powdered gelatine)
100g/4oz sultanas • 3 tbsps rum
50g/2oz each candied lemon and orange peel
50g/2oz shelled walnuts
100g/4oz chocolate flake
1 vanilla pod
250ml/8 fl oz milk
4 eggs • 3 tbsps sugar
200ml/6 fl oz whipping cream
100g/4oz sponge fingers
125 ml/4 fl oz cooled, strong black coffee
400ml/15 fl oz Amaretto

Preparation time: 1 hour
Chilling time: 1 hour
Nutritional value:
Analysis per serving, approx:
• 1700kJ/405kcal
• 11g protein
• 32g fat
• 35g carbohydrate

Soak the leaf gelatine in the cold water. • Marinate the sultanas in the rum • Chop peel and nuts, and mix with half the chocolate flake. • Split the vanilla pod, scrape out the inside, add both to the milk and heat. • Separate the eggs. • Beat the egg yolks with the sugar over a pan of simmering water until fluffy. • Remove the vanilla pod, add the milk slowly to the yolks and heat the mixture for 4 minutes over the pan of simmering water. • Squeeze out the leaf gelatine (if using powdered gelatine, follow the directions on the packet) and mix with the warm egg yolk mixture. • Beat the egg whites until stiff and refrigerate. Beat the cream. Fold in the whipped cream and lastly the egg whites. • Put half this mixture into a glass serving bowl. Arrange the sponge fingers on top and sprinkle with the coffee and Amaretto. Next add the sultanas and peel mixture, and lastly the remaining mixture.

Hot Puddings

Classic and new desserts from oven or pan,
boiled, deep-fried, flambéed. . .
temptingly served with fruit
and delicious sauces

Clafoutis

A cherry soufflé from the Limoges region of France

75g/3oz flour

3 eggs

200ml/6 fl oz milk

2 tbsps butter

500g/1lb 2oz black cherries, stoned

Pinch of salt

4 tbsps sugar

Butter for the dish

Preparation time: 1 hour
Cooking time: 45 minutes
Nutritional value:

Analysis per serving, approx:
- 2000kJ/480kcal
- 15g protein
- 22g fat
- 54g carbohydrate

Heat the oven to 190°C/375°F/Gas Mark 5. Sift the flour into a bowl. • Separate one of the eggs. • Add the egg yolk and the other eggs into the flour and gradually add the milk to make a smooth batter. • Melt the butter and gradually stir it into the batter. • Leave the batter covered at room temperature for 30 minutes. • Wash the cherries and and pat dry. • Butter a shallow, ovenproof dish. • Beat the egg white with the salt until stiff and fold into the batter. • Pour the batter into the baking dish, arrange the cherries on top and allow them to sink in. • Bake the clafoutis on the middle shelf of the oven for 20 minutes. Sprinkle the clafoutis with the sugar and bake for a further 20 minutes. • Turn off the oven and leave the soufflé to stand in it for a further five minutes.

Desserts from the Oven

Combined with a vegetable soup to start, these make a filling lunch

Carrot Pancakes
top left

FOR THE PANCAKES:

50g/2oz shelled hazelnuts

200g/7oz carrots

50g/2oz wholemeal flour

3 eggs

50g/2oz honey

125ml/4 fl oz milk

Juice and grated rind of ½ a lemon

15g/1oz butter

FOR THE SAUCE:

100g/4oz quark or low-fat curd cheese

100ml/3 fl oz single cream

1 tbsp orange blossom honey

Pinch of ground cloves

1 tsp grated orange peel

2 oranges

Preparation time: 1¼ hours
Nutritional value:
Analysis per serving, approx:

- 2100kJ/500kcal
- 19g protein
- 30g fat
- 39g carbohydrate

Roast the hazelnuts in a dry frying pan and allow to cool. Remove the brown skins by rubbing the nuts in a kitchen towel. Chop the nuts finely. • Wash, peel and grate the carrots and mix with the flour, nuts, eggs, honey and milk. • Leave the dough to rest for 10 minutes, then mix with the lemon juice and rind. • Turn the oven to its lowest setting. • Melt the butter and make 8 pancakes with the batter, frying each for 3 minutes per side. Keep the pancakes warm in the oven. • Mix the quark with the cream, honey, ground cloves and orange peel. • Peel the oranges and separate them into sections. • Serve the sauce and the orange segments with the pancakes.

Fluffy Millet Tarts
top right

80g/3oz millet

250ml/8 fl oz water

80ml/3 fl oz double cream

3 tbsps runny honey

30g/1 oz butter

1 tsp grated lemon rind

½ tsp vanilla essence

3 eggs

100g/4oz raspberries

4 tbsps maple or golden syrup

Preparation time: 30 minutes
Cooking time: 1 hour
Nutritional value:
Analysis per serving, approx:

- 1400kJ/330kcal
- 13g protein
- 19g fat
- 32g carbohydrate

Place the millet and water in a pan, cover and simmer gently for 20 minutes. Turn off the heat and leave for a further 10 minutes. • Drain the millet, mix it with the cream and leave it to stand away from the heat for a further 10 minutes. • Mix 2 tbsps honey, the butter, lemon rind and vanilla into the millet. • Separate the eggs. • Add the egg yolks to the millet mixture. Whisk the egg whites and the remaining honey until stiff and fold into the millet. • Turn the oven to its lowest setting. • Melt some butter in a saucepan with a lid. Shape the millet mixture into four small cakes and spread the raspberries on top. Cover the pan and cook the cakes for about 10 minutes over a low heat. • Transfer to a buttered, warm serving dish and keep in the oven until ready to serve. • Sprinkle with syrup just before serving.

Traditional Steamed Puddings

Serve these traditional puddings with custard

Chocolate Pudding
top left

Ingredients for 10 people:
200g/7oz unblanched almonds
250g/8oz plain chocolate
¹/₂ vanilla pod
75g/3oz softened butter
200g/7oz sugar
8 eggs
3 tbsps breadcrumbs
1 tsp ground cinnamon

Preparation time: 40 minutes
Cooking time: 1¹/₂ hours
Nutritional value:
Analysis per serving, approx:
- 2400kJ/570kcal
- 17g protein
- 36g fat
- 46g carbohydrate

Scald the almonds in boiling water, drain the water and remove the skins. • Grind the almonds. • Grate the chocolate. Split the vanilla pod and scrape out the vanilla. • Cream the butter and sugar until fluffy. • Separate the eggs. Gradually stir the yolks into the butter and sugar mixture. • Stir the almonds, chocolate, vanilla, breadcrumbs and cinnamon into the egg yolks. • Whisk the egg whites until stiff and fold them into the mixture. • Butter a mould or pudding basin and fill it with the chocolate mixture. • Cover the mould tightly with a lid or cloth and place it in a pan of boiling water filled to 5cm/2in below the top. • Simmer the pudding for 1¹/₂ hours. • Leave it to cool slightly, then turn out and serve while it is still warm.

Bread Pudding
top right

Ingredients for 6 people:
8 stale bread rolls or 400g/14oz stale white bread
250ml/8 fl oz milk
6 eggs
100g/4oz sugar
150g/5¹/₂oz softened butter
1 lemon
150g/5¹/₂oz raisins
50g/2oz candied lemon peel
100g/4oz ground almonds
1 tsp ground cinnamon
2 tbsps semolina

Preparation time: 30 minutes
Cooking time: 1¹/₂ hours
Nutritional value:
Analysis per serving, approx:
- 3100kJ/740kcal
- 17g protein
- 44g fat
- 78g carbohydrate

Cut the bread rolls or bread into small pieces and soak in the milk. • Separate the eggs. Cream the sugar and butter until fluffy and gradually beat in the egg yolks. • Squeeze out the softened bread and stir into the egg yolk mixture. • Wash the lemon in warm water, dry it and grate the rind finely. • Rinse the raisins in hot water and pat them dry. • Dice the candied lemon peel finely. • Combine the lemon peel, the raisins, candied lemon peel, almonds, cinnamon and semolina with the bread. • Whisk the egg whites until stiff and fold them into the pudding mixture. • Butter the mould, fill it three-quarters full with the pudding and cover. • Place in a saucepan of boiling water filled to 5 cm/2in below the lid. • Simmer the pudding on a low heat for 1¹/₂ hours. • Leave the pudding to cool slightly, then unmould it and serve hot.

Salzburg Soufflé

A delight which melts on the tongue

3 eggs
2 egg whites
Pinch of salt
3 tbsps sugar
3 tbsps flour, sifted
Grated rind of ½ lemon
1 tbsp vanilla sugar
30g/1oz butter
5 tbsps milk

Preparation time: 15 minutes
Cooking time: 5 minutes
Nutritional value:
Analysis per serving, approx:
• 1200kJ/290kcal
• 16g protein
• 15g fat
• 17g carbohydrate

Heat the oven to 220°C/425°F/Gas Mark 7. • Separate the 3 eggs. Whisk all egg whites with the salt until stiff, then continue whisking whilst slowly adding the sugar. • Whisk the egg yolks with the sifted flour, lemon rind and vanilla sugar and fold in the beaten egg whites. • Melt the butter in a shallow, oval gratin dish and add the milk. • Using a spatula, shape four dumplings from the egg white mixture and arrange them in the dish. Each dumpling should have a small peak. • Place the dish on the middle shelf of the oven and bake for about five minutes until the peaks are slightly browned. • Serve immediately, in the baking dish, before the dumplings have a chance to collapse.

Apple-Rice Soufflé

A complete meal when served with a salad hors d'oeuvre

Ingredients for 6 people:
500ml/16 fl oz milk
Pinch of salt
150g/5½oz short-grain rice
4 tbsps raisins
1 tsp rum
3 eggs
100g/4oz softened butter
100g/4oz sugar
1 tsp grated lemon rind
2 tsps vanilla sugar
3 medium apples
1 tsp lemon juice
6 tsps raspberry jam
Butter for the baking dish

Preparation time: 1 hour
Cooking time: 45 minutes
Nutritional value:
Analysis per serving, approx:
• 2000kJ/470kcal
• 11g protein
• 22g fat
• 58g carbohydrate

Add the salt to the milk and bring to the boil. Add the rice to the milk, stir and cook on a gentle heat for 15 minutes. Remove from the heat; then plunge in a container of cold water to cool completely; leave to stand for another 15 minutes. • Wash the raisins in lukewarm water, pat dry and marinate in the rum. • Separate the eggs and beat the yolks with the butter, sugar, lemon rind and vanilla sugar until the mixture is fluffy. • Add the rice and raisins. • Whisk the egg whites until stiff and fold into the rice pudding. • Heat the oven to 200°C/400°F/Gas Mark 6. Butter a baking dish and fill it with the rice mixture. • Wash, halve and core the apples; brush them with the lemon juice and arrange them on the rice. • Bake the soufflé on the middle shelf of the oven for 45 minutes. • Before serving, spoon jam over the apples.

Desserts from the Frying Pan

Delightful and unusual pancake mixtures

Viennese Emperor Pancake
top left

Ingredients for 6 people:

4 eggs

250g/8oz flour

250ml/8 fl oz milk

Pinch of salt

1 heaped tbsp sugar

1 tbsp vanilla sugar

100g/4oz raisins

100g/4oz butter

50g/2oz icing sugar, sifted

Preparation time: 30 minutes
Nutritional value:

Analysis per serving, approx:
- 2330kJ/500kcal
- 14g protein
- 23g fat
- 57g carbohydrate

Separate the eggs. • Beat the flour into the egg yolks and milk. • Whisk the egg whites with the salt and continue beating, while gradually adding the sugar and vanilla sugar, until stiff. Fold into the yolk mixture. • Wash the raisins in hot water and pat dry. • Melt half the butter in a large pan, add the pancake mixture and scatter raisins over it. • When the mixture is golden-brown on the underside but still liquid on top, turn it and add the remaining butter. • Once the underside is again golden-brown, break up the pancake with two forks. • Cook the pancake for a further five minutes over a gentle heat, turning when necessary. • Place on a warm plate and sprinkle generously with sifted icing sugar. • In Vienna, the pancake is served with plums stewed in a little white wine and cinnamon.

Cherry Pancakes
top right

125ml/4 fl oz milk

2 eggs

1 tbsp vanilla sugar

Pinch of salt

75g/3oz caster sugar

125g/5oz flour

300g/10oz black cherries

200ml/6 fl oz whipping cream

1/2 vanilla pod

30g/1oz clarified butter

4 tbsps maraschino liqueur

2 tbsps icing sugar, sifted

Preparation time: 1 1/4 hours
Nutritional value:

Analysis per serving, approx:
- 2500kJ/600kcal
- 13g protein
- 27g fat
- 66g carbohydrate

Whisk the milk with the eggs, vanilla sugar, salt and 50g/2oz sugar. • Sift the flour into the mixture and stir well. Cover and leave the batter to stand for 30 minutes. • Wash and stone the cherries. • Whip the cream until it forms soft peaks. • Split the vanilla pod, scrape out the vanilla, mix it with the remaining sugar and stir into the cream. Whip the cream until stiff and chill it. • Turn the oven to its lowest setting. • Mix the cherries with the batter and use the clarified butter to fry eight small pancakes. • Keep the finished pancakes warm in the oven. • Arrange them on warmed dishes, sprinkle with the liqueur and then with sifted icing sugar. Serve with the vanilla cream sauce.

Our Tip: For special occasions, serve with lemon sorbet or pistachio ice cream.

Delicious Omelettes

There are numerous possibilities here for variations on the theme

Lemon Omelettes
top left

3 eggs	
Pinch of salt	
75g/3oz caster sugar	
3 tbsps vanilla sugar	
75g/3oz flour	
75g/3oz cornflour	
1 lemon	
250ml/8 fl oz whipping cream	
125g/5oz icing sugar, sifted	

Preparation time: 40 minutes
Nutritional value:
Analysis per serving, approx:
- 2900kJ/690kcal
- 15g protein
- 29g fat
- 90g carbohydrate

Heat the oven to180°C/
350°F/Gas Mark 4. •
Separate the eggs. Whisk the egg
whites with the salt and gradually
add 50g/2oz caster sugar until the
mixture stands in stiff peaks. •
Whisk the yolks with 1 tbsp hot
water and the rest of the sugar
and the vanilla sugar until fluffy. •
Sift the flour and cornflour into the
egg yolks, mix well, then fold in
the egg whites. • Line a baking tin
with lightly greased baking
parchment. Spread the mixture
over it and bake for 12 to 15
minutes until golden-brown. •
Rinse the lemon, dry, peel very
finely and cut the rind into
julienne strips. Squeeze out the
lemon juice and reserve. •
Sprinkle a tea towel with icing
sugar, turn out the baked omelette
onto it and remove the paper. •
Cut out four circles about
14cm/6in in diameter. Fold these
omelettes in half and cover with a
damp cloth. Reserve in a warm
place. • Whip the cream with
100g/4oz icing sugar, lemon juice
and rind until stiff. • Pipe the
lemon cream into the folded
omelettes and sift over the icing
sugar.

Sponge Omelette with Jam
top right

15g/¹/₂oz butter	
5 eggs	
3 tbsps sugar	
2 tbsps vanilla sugar	
4 tbsps flour	
2 tsps grated lemon rind	
Pinch of salt	
4 tbsps apricot jam	
3 tbsps orange liqueur	
2 tbsps icing sugar, sifted	

Preparation time: 35 minutes
Nutritional value:
Analysis per serving, approx:
- 1500kJ/360kcal
- 17g protein
- 17g fat
- 32g carbohydrate

Heat the oven to
180°C/350°F/Gas Mark 4.
Melt the butter in a shallow, round
30cm/12 inch cake tin, ensuring
that the base is evenly coated. •
Separate the eggs. Whisk the
whites until stiff and, while still
whisking, gradually add the sugar
and vanilla sugar. • Add the flour,
lemon rind and salt to the egg
yolks and fold in the egg whites
with a mixing spoon. • Transfer
the sponge mixture to the cake tin,
making the edges a little thicker
than the centre. • Bake on the
middle shelf of the oven for about
15 minutes until golden. • Warm
the apricot jam with the liqueur,
stirring constantly. • Turn the
omelette onto a plate, spread half
with the preserve and fold the
other half over it. Sprinkle with
sifted icing sugar and cut into four
portions.

The Most Popular Crêpes

Oranges may be substituted for mandarines, and lemon or lime marmalade for orange

Crêpes Suzette
top left

45g/1½oz butter
125g/5oz flour
1 egg
1 egg yolk
2 tbsps sugar
Pinch of salt
250ml/8 fl oz milk
75g/3oz softened butter
2 tbsps icing sugar
3 mandarins or satsumas, rinsed
1 heaped tbsp sugar
4 tbsps curaçao
2 tbsps cognac
45g/1½oz clarified butter

Preparation time: 1½ hours
Nutritional value:
Analysis per serving, approx:
• 2800kJ/670kcal
• 13g protein
• 42g fat
• 49g carbohydrate

Melt 30g/1oz of the butter. •
Mix the flour with the egg,
egg yolk, sugar, salt, milk and ½oz
butter. • Turn the oven to its
lowest setting. • Melt the clarified
butter in portions in a small, heavy
crêpe pan. Make 12 very thin
crêpes and keep them warm in the
oven. • Cream the softened butter
and icing sugar until fluffy. •
Finely grate the rind off the
satsumas. Squeeze out the juice. •
Mix half the satsuma rind and
juice into the creamed butter. •
Mix the other half of the juice and
rind with the sugar and reserve. •
Mix the curaçao with the cognac.
• Brush the crêpes with the
flavoured butter, fold into quarters
and arrange in a buttered crêpe
pan. • Pour the juice over the
crêpes and heat, allowing the juice
to run under the crêpes. • As soon
as the juice has thickened a little,
add the alcohol, ignite and serve
the crêpes immediately, while still
alight.

Orange Crêpes
top right

100g/4oz butter
100g/4oz flour
Scant 250ml/8 fl oz milk
Pinch of salt
1 tbsp sugar
2 eggs
Generous pinch of ground cinnamon
Rind of ½ orange
200g/7oz bitter orange marmalade
1 tbsp orange liqueur

Preparation time: 1¼ hours
Nutritional value:
Analysis per serving, approx:
• 2300kJ/550kcal
• 11g protein
• 29g fat
• 58g carbohydrate

Melt 30g/1oz of the butter and
allow to cool. • Blend the
flour with the milk, salt, melted
butter and sugar. • Whisk the eggs
and cinnamon and mix into the
batter. • Cover and leave to stand
for 30 minutes. • Wash the
orange in warm water, dry, peel
very thinly and cut the rind into
fine strips. • Mix the marmalade
with the liqueur. • Use the rest of
the butter and the batter to cook
eight very thin crêpes, using a
crêpe pan or other small pan. To
flip the crêpes over, turn them
onto a lid or plate and then slide
back into the pan. Cook for 2
minutes on each side or until
golden-brown. • Turn the oven to
its lowest setting. • Spread the
finished crêpes with the
marmalade, fold twice and keep
warm in the oven. • Sprinkle with
orange rind and serve.

Sophisticated Sweet Crêpes

Fruit-filled pancakes make a hearty snack all by themselves

Calvados Crêpes Flambées
top left

FOR THE BATTER:

100g/4oz flour
125ml/4 fl oz milk
Pinch of salt
3 tbsps single cream
1 tbsp vanilla sugar
2 eggs
Grated rind of ½ lemon

FOR THE FILLING:

500g/1lb 2oz small tart apples
Juice of ½ lemon
100g/4oz butter
2 tbsps sugar
½ tsp ground cinnamon
6 tbsps Calvados
1 tsp cornflour
50g/2oz chopped hazelnuts

Preparation time: 1½ hours
Nutritional value:
Analysis per serving, approx:

- 2200kJ/520kcal
- 13g protein
- 28g fat
- 48g carbohydrate

Mix all ingredients for the batter and leave, covered, for 30 minutes. • Turn the oven to its lowest setting. • Wash and core the apples, cut into 1-cm/½-inch slices and sprinkle with lemon juice. • Melt 15g/½oz of the butter in a saucepan. Add the apples, sugar, cinnamon and 4 tbsps Calvados. Stew, covered, for 5 minutes. • Blend the cornflour with a little cold water, mix into the apples and return to the boil. Remove from the heat and sprinkle with nuts. • Make 12 small crêpes with the batter and the rest of the butter. • Fill the finished crêpes with the apples, fold and keep warm in the oven. • Heat the rest of the Calvados gently. Pour over the crêpes, ignite and serve.

Crêpes with Strawberry Cream
top right

FOR THE BATTER:

125g/5oz flour • 2 eggs
200ml/7 fl oz milk
2 tbsps oil
1 tbsp vanilla sugar • Pinch of salt

FOR THE FILLING:

300g/10oz strawberries
Juice of ½ lemon
100ml/3 fl oz whipping cream
2 tbsps sugar
1 tbsp vanilla sugar
3 tbsps clarified butter
2 tbsps icing sugar, sfited

Preparation time: 1½ hours
Nutritional value:
Analysis per serving, approx:
- 2200kJ/530kcal
- 13g protein
- 31g fat
- 48g carbohydrate

Mix all the ingredients for the batter; cover and leave to stand for 30 minutes. • Wash, dry and hull the strawberries. • Take a third of the strawberries and cut each into quarters; pass the rest through a fine sieve and mix with the lemon juice. • Whip the cream with the sugar and vanilla sugar until stiff and fold in the strawberry purée and quarters. Place in the refrigerator. • Turn the oven to its lowest setting. • Use the clarified butter and batter to make eight very thin crêpes. • To flip the crêpes, turn them out onto a plate and slide them back into the pan, cooking for 2 minutes on each side until golden-brown. • Keep the finished crêpes warm. • Divide the strawberry cream between the crêpes, fold into quarters and sprinkle with the sifted icing sugar.

Sweet Cheese Pancakes

A deliciously different dessert

Sweet Pancakes with Nut Cream

A particularly sophisticated variation on the pancake theme

FOR THE BATTER:

125g/5oz flour • Pinch of salt

2 eggs • 1 tbsp oil

250ml/8 fl oz milk

1 tsp vanilla sugar

FOR THE FILLING:

250g/8oz quark

50g/2oz softened butter

50g/2oz sugar • 2 egg yolks

1/2 tsp grated lemon rind

5 tbsps sour cream

75g/3oz raisins, washed

3 egg whites

1 tbsp vanilla sugar

FOR THE GLAZE:

125ml/4 fl oz milk

1 egg yolk • 1 tsp sugar

100g/4oz butter

For topping: 2 tbsps sugar

1 tsp ground cinnamon

Preparation time: 1¼ hours
Cooking time: 30 minutes
Nutritional value:

Analysis per serving, approx:
- 3700kJ/880kcal
- 32g protein
- 53g fat
- 66g carbohydrate

Mix all ingredients for the batter, cover and leave to stand for 30 minutes. • Drain the quark in a sieve. • Cream butter and sugar until fluffy. Combine the egg yolks with the lemon rind, quark, sour cream and raisins and add to the creamed butter mix. • Whisk the egg whites with the vanilla sugar until stiff and fold into the quark mixture. • Melt a little butter and cook eight thin pancakes. • Heat the oven to 180°C/350°F/Gas Mark 4. • Spread some of the mixture over each pancake, roll up, cut in half and place in a buttered dish, overlapping one another. • Whisk the milk, egg yolk and sugar and pour over the pancakes. Bake for 30 mins. Sprinkle with the cinnamon and sugar mixture and serve.

FOR THE BATTER:

150g/5½oz flour

Pinch of salt

2 eggs

1 egg yolk

250ml/8 fl oz milk

FOR THE FILLING:

100g/4oz plain chocolate

200ml/6 fl oz whipping cream

1 egg white

1 tbsp vanilla sugar

1 tbsp rum

150g/5½oz ground hazelnuts

FOR COOKING: 75g/3oz butter

Preparation time: 1 hour
Nutritional value:

Analysis per serving, approx:
- 3600kJ/860kcal
- 24g protein
- 59g fat
- 54g carbohydrate

Make a batter with the flour, salt, eggs, egg yolk and milk. Cover and leave to stand for 30 minutes. • Meanwhile, melt the chocolate over a pan of simmering water and stir in 5 tbsps of the cream. • Whip the rest of the cream until stiff. • Whisk the egg white with the vanilla sugar until stiff and fold into the hazelnuts; add the rum. • Fold half the whipped cream into the nut mixture. • Turn the oven to its lowest setting. • Use the butter and batter to make eight thin pancakes, cooking over a medium heat and turning every two to three minutes, until golden-brown. • Keep the finished pancakes warm in the oven until all the batter is used up. • Brush the pancakes with the melted chocolate, spread the nuts and cream on top and roll them up. • Decorate the pancakes with the rest of the whipped cream and serve on warm plates.

Rhubarb Flans with Mango Sauce

An outstanding dessert

Ingredients for four small soufflé dishes:

250g/8oz young rhubarb
Grated rind of ¹/₂ a lemon
75g/3oz sugar
¹/₂ tsp ground ginger
8 sponge fingers
75g/3oz ground hazelnuts
3 eggs
1 ripe mango
Juice of ¹/₂ lemon
125ml/4 fl oz mango syrup

Preparation time: 1¹/₂ hours
Cooking time: 35 minutes
Nutritional value:
Analysis per serving, approx:
- 2300kJ/550kcal
- 15g protein
- 32g fat
- 51g carbohydrate

Wash and dry the rhubarb, trim it and remove the strings. • Cut it into 2-cm/³/₄-inch chunks, sprinkle with the lemon rind, half the sugar and the ginger. Cover and leave at room temperature for one hour. • Crush the sponge fingers between cling film using a rolling pin and mix with the nuts. • Heat the oven to 180°C/350°F/Gas Mark 4. Butter two flan tins and add about a quarter of the nut-and-sponge mixture. • Separate the eggs. Whisk the egg whites until stiff, slowly adding the rest of the sugar and ginger and continue to whisk for another two minutes. • Drain the rhubarb and fold into the egg yolks with the rest of the nut-and-sponge mixture. Lastly, fold in the egg whites and transfer to the flan tins. Place the flan tins in a baking tin half-filled with boiling water. Bake the flans on the middle shelf of the oven for about 35 minutes. • Peel the mango. Cut the flesh away from the stone, slice and purée it in a mixer with the lemon juice and the mango syrup. Serve the sauce separately with the flans.

Fruit in Batter

Particularly appealing in winter

Pineapple Fritters
top left

150g/5¹/₂oz flour	
2 eggs	
Pinch of salt	
125ml/4 fl oz milk	
1 tbsp rosewater	
1 tbsp vanilla sugar	
1 small pineapple	
Oil for deep frying	

FOR DUSTING:

3 tbsps sugar	
¹/₂ tsp ground cinnamon	

Preparation time: 1 hour
Nutritional value:
Analysis per serving, approx:
• 2700kJ/640kcal
• 13g protein
• 32g fat
• 73g carbohydrate

To make the batter, mix the flour with the eggs, salt, milk, rosewater and vanilla sugar. •

Cover, and leave the batter to stand for 30 minutes. • Peel the pineapple, cut into 1-cm/¹/₂-inch-thick slices, discarding the woody core. • Heat the oil to 180°C/350°F in a deep fryer or saucepan; using a sugar or frying thermometer to check the temperature. • Stir the batter again and, using a fork, dip the pineapple slices in the batter, allow to drain a little and fry in batches in the hot oil until golden-brown on both sides. • Turn the oven to its lowest setting and keep the finished pineapple slices warm until all have been cooked. • Mix the sugar and cinnamon and sprinkle this over the pineapple before serving.

Our Tip: For a richer dessert with a Christmas flavour, pour 100g/4oz crème fraîche mixed with egg nog onto the pineapple slices instead of cinnamon sugar.

Apple Fritters Flambées
top right

100g/4oz flour	
2 eggs	
Pinch of salt	
2 tsps vanilla sugar	
4-5 tbsps milk	
3 medium apples	
2 tsps butter	
2 tbsps sugar	
¹/₂ tsp ground cinnamon	
4 tbsps dark rum	
Oil for deep frying	

Preparation time: 1 hour
Nutritional value:
Analysis per serving, approx:
• 2200kJ/520kcal
• 10g protein
• 34g fat
• 40g carbohydrate

Mix the flour with the eggs, salt and vanilla sugar and add enough milk to make a thick batter. Cover and leave to rest for 30 minutes. • Heat the oil to 175°C/337°F, either in a deep fryer or a saucepan, using a sugar thermometer to check the temperature. • Peel and core the apples with an apple corer and cut each into four thick rings. • Dip the rings in the batter using a fork and fry three or four at a time in the oil until golden, turning once. • Drain the fritters on absorbent paper. • Melt the butter. Mix with the sugar and cinnamon and fry the apple fritters on each side until the sugar has browned slightly. Pour the rum over the fritters and set it alight. Serve the fritters immediately, while still flaming.

Viennese Apple Strudel

Every Viennese lady swears by her own family recipe for strudel – ours comes from an old Viennese recipe book

Ingredients for 8 portions:

FOR THE DOUGH:

250g/8oz flour
2 tsps oil
Pinch of salt
1 small egg
100ml/3 fl oz lukewarm water

FOR THE FILLING:

50g/2oz butter
2 tbsps breadcrumbs
2kg/4¹/₂lbs cooking apples
Juice of ¹/₂ lemon
75g/3oz raisins
100g/4oz almonds
75g/3oz sugar
Penerous pinch of ground cinnamon

Preparation time: 1¹/₄ hours
Baking time: 40 minutes
Nutritional value:

Analysis per serving, approx:
• 2200kJ/520kcal
• 9g protein
• 26g fat
• 64g carbohydrate per serving

Sift the flour onto a board or marble slab, make a well in the centre and pour in the oil, salt and egg. Knead the dough, using enough lukewarm water to make it smooth and supple. • Knead until the dough separates from the working surface easily and is glossy; this takes about 10 minutes. If the ball of dough is sliced through, it should show clear rings. • Reshape the dough into a ball, brush with a little oil and leave to rest under an inverted bowl for no longer than 30 minutes. • To make the filling, melt 50g/2oz of the butter, fry the breadcrumbs in it until golden-brown and set aside. • Quarter the apples, peel and core them and cut into slices; sprinkle with lemon juice. • Wash the raisins in hot water and allow to drain. • Scald the almonds in boiling water, remove the skins and chop them coarsely. • Mix the sugar and cinnamon. • Place a 120x80cm/50inx30in cloth on the work surface and sprinkle it with flour. • Roll out the dough on the cloth into a wide rectangle and brush this with oil. • Starting from the middle, roll out the dough in all directions until paper-thin, trimming any thick edges. • Heat the oven to 200°C/400°F/Gas Mark 6. Brush a baking sheet with melted butter. • Spread the breadcrumbs over the dough, leaving a 10-cm/4-inch wide margin free along one of the long edges. • Scatter the apple pieces over the breadcrumbs, then add the raisins and chopped almonds. Finally sprinkle with the cinnamon sugar. • With the help of the cloth, roll the strudel towards the free edge and lay it on the baking sheet, forming a horseshoe shape. The seam should be underneath. • Brush the strudel with melted butter and bake on the middle shelf of the oven for 40 minutes until golden-brown. During baking, brush the strudel with melted butter at 10-minute intervals. • Allow the strudel to cool slightly under a cloth. • Cut it into portions while still warm.

Our Tip: Cold apple strudel is delicious as coffee cake or at teatime. If it is too sour it can be sprinkled with cinnamon sugar or sifted icing sugar.

Blood Orange Soufflé

A festive soufflé to serve with fruit

3 blood oranges
3 navel oranges
2 lemons
8 sugar cubes
6 tbsps Grand Marnier
6 sponge fingers
6 eggs
100g/4oz sugar
Butter and sugar for the tin

Preparation time: 1 hour
Baking: 25 minutes
Nutritional value:

Analysis per serving, approx:
- 2500kJ/600kcal
- 23g protein
- 21g fat
- 70g carbohydrate

Peel the blood oranges like an apple, using a sharp knife, and discard the white pith. Divide them into segments, removing the skins, and set aside. Squeeze the navel oranges and reserve the juice. • Wash the lemons in warm water, dry them and rub the peel with the sugar cubes. • Squeeze the lemons and boil the juice with that of the oranges and the sugar cubes until a thickened syrup forms. • Sprinkle the orange segments with half the liqueur, cover and set aside. • Brush a soufflé dish with butter and sprinkle with sugar. • Arrange the sponge fingers in the dish and sprinkle the rest of the liqueur over them. • Heat the oven to 250°C/500°F/Gas Mark 9. • Separate the eggs. Stir the sugar into the egg yolks and then beat over a pan of hot water until fluffy. • Mix the fruit syrup with the yolk mixture and stir over a pan of cold water until cool. • Whisk the egg whites until stiff, fold into the egg yolk mixture and pour into the dish. • Bake for about 10 minutes on the middle shelf of the oven, then reduce the temperature to 200°C/400°F/Gas Mark 6. Bake the soufflé for a further 15 minutes. • Serve immediately or it will collapse quickly. Serve the orange segments as an accompaniment.

Baked Puddings

Both desserts should be baked immediately prior to serving

Berry Gratin
top left

| 400g/14oz mixed berries |
| 1/4 vanilla pod |
| 4 egg yolks |
| 75g/3oz sugar |
| Grated rind of 1/2 a lemon |
| 125ml/4 fl oz sherry |
| 50g/2oz blanched ground almonds |
| 4 scoops of strawberry sorbet |

Preparation time: 30 minutes
Browning time: 4 to 8 minutes
Nutritional value:
Analysis per serving, approx:
• 2900kJ/690kcal
• 21g protein
• 44g fat
• 38g carbohydrate

Wash the berries and leave to drain. • Place three-quarters of the berries in individual ovenproof dishes. Cover the rest and reserve. • Heat the oven to 220°C/425°F/Gas Mark 7. • Split the vanilla pod and scrape out the vanilla. Beat the egg yolks with the vanilla, sugar, lemon rind and sherry over a pan of simmering water until creamy. The mixture should become hot. Fold in the almonds. • Pour the mixture over the berries and bake until golden on the middle shelf of the oven for 4 to 8 minutes. • Decorate the dessert with the remaining berries and serve with a scoop of the sorbet.

Vanilla Soufflé
top right

| 500g/1lb 2oz raspberries |
| 1 tbsp raspberry liqueur |
| 100g/4oz sugar |
| 5 eggs |
| 1 vanilla pod |
| Pinch of salt |
| 50g/2oz flour |
| 30g/1oz cornflour |
| 1 tbsp sour cream |
| 2 tbsps lemon juice |
| 1 tsp grated lemon rind |
| Butter and sugar for the dish |
| 1 tbsp icing sugar to dust |

Preparation time: 40 minutes
Baking: 35 minutes
Nutritional value:
Analysis per serving, approx:
• 1900kJ/450kcal
• 19g protein
• 17g fat
• 55g carbohydrate

Wash the raspberries and leave to drain; mix with the raspberry liqueur and 2 tbsps sugar. • Heat the oven to 180°C/350°F/Gas Mark 4. Butter a soufflé dish and sprinkle with sugar. • Separate the eggs. • Split the vanilla pod, scrape out the vanilla and mix into the egg yolks with half the remaining sugar; beat until fluffy. • Whisk the egg whites with the salt and gradually add the remaining sugar, continuing to beat until stiff. • Mix the flour and all but 1 tsp of the cornflour and stir, with the sour cream, into the egg yolk mixture. Fold in the egg whites. • Put half the beaten mixture into the dish, spread 250g/8oz drained raspberries on top and cover with the remaining mixture. • Bake the soufflé in the middle of the oven for 35 minutes until golden-brown. • Cook the remaining raspberries with the juice, the lemon juice and rind as well as 125ml/4 fl oz water, for five minutes, then add the 1 tsp cornflour mixed with a little cold water and bring to the boil again. • Sift icing sugar over the soufflé and serve immediately with the raspberry sauce.

Pies – Surprises beneath a Delicate Crust

American pies – sweet and tasty, hot and cold

Chiffon Pie
top left

Ingredients for a 24-cm/10-inch flan dish:

100g/4oz nut paste
8 rusks
100g/4oz marzipan
1 tsp ground ginger
5 leaves or 2 tsps powdered gelatine
250ml/8 fl oz water
250ml/8 fl oz orange juice
Grated rind of 1 orange
Juice of 1 lemon
4 eggs
100g/4oz sugar
200ml/6 fl oz whipping cream
4 tbsps orange liqueur
1 tbsp chopped pistachios

Preparation time: 1¹/₂ hours
Cooling: 2 hours
Nutritional value:
Analysis per serving (serves 8):
• 1700kJ/400kcal
• 11g protein
• 21g fat
• 42g carbohydrate

Melt the nut paste over a pan of simmering water. • Remove from the heat. Crush the rusks. • Mix the marzipan with the paste, rusks and ginger. • Line the base and edges of a pie dish with this mixture and cool for one hour. • Soak the gelatine leaves in the water. • Boil the orange juice and rind and the lemon juice. • Separate the eggs. Mix 50g/2oz sugar with the egg yolks over a pan of simmering water until creamy. • Squeeze the liquid from the gelatine and dissolve in the fruit juice, (if using powdered, follow directions on packet) and stir into the egg yolk mixture. Leave to cool. • Whisk the egg whites and the rest of the sugar until stiff. • Whip the cream until stiff and stir in the liqueur. • Fold the egg whites and whipped cream into the mixture as it starts to set, place in the pie dish and refrigerate for at least two hours.

Pecan Pie
top right

Ingredients for a 24cm/10-in pie:

150g/5¹/₂oz cold butter
300g/10oz flour
Pinch of salt
1 egg yolk
For the filling:
4 eggs
300g/10oz golden syrup
40g/1¹/₂oz flour
60g/2oz butter
1 tsp vanilla essence
400g/14oz pecan nuts, halved

Preparation time: 45 minutes
Baking: 30 minutes
Nutritional value:
Analysis per serving (serves 10):
• 3230kJ/770kcal
• 27g protein
• 58g fat
• 76g carbohydrate

Make a shortcrust pastry with the butter, flour and salt, egg yolk and about 2 tbsps of cold water. • Cover and leave in the refrigerator for 30 minutes to rest. • Heat the oven to180°C/350°F/ Gas Mark 4. • Whisk the eggs and stir in the syrup. • Stir the flour, melted butter, vanilla and nuts into the syrup. • Roll out the dough and cut out 2 circles of 24 and 28 cm/10 and 11 ins in diameter respectively. • Line the flan dish with the larger circle of pastry. • Fill with the nut mixture, cover with the smaller circle and press the edges together. • Cut a star shape in the middle of the pie top and fold the points of the star back so that the nut filling is visible. • Bake the pie for 30 minutes.

Apples and Apricots served Hot

Caramelising the sugar gives these cooked fruits an unusual flavour

Baked Apples Flambé
top left

4 large cooking apples	
100g/4oz sultanas	
2 tbsps rum	
50g/2oz chopped hazelnuts	
125g/5oz marzipan	
Generous pinch of ground cinnamon	
1 tbsp vanilla sugar	
½ lemon	
4 tbsps Calvados or cognac	

Preparation time: 20 minutes
Baking: 30 minutes
Nutritional value:
Analysis per serving, approx:
• 1700kJ/400kcal
• 5g protein
• 15g fat
• 56g carbohydrate

Heat the oven to 200°C/400°F/Gas Mark 6. Line a baking tin with baking parchment • Wash, dry and core the apples, using a corer. • Rinse the sultanas in hot water, pat dry and mix with the rum and chopped hazelnuts. • Dice the marzipan, mix with cinnamon and vanilla sugar and then add to the sultanas. • Rinse the lemon in warm water, dry it, grate the rind and squeeze out the juice. • Mix the juice and rind with the marzipan mixture. • Fill the apples with this mixture, place on the baking sheet and bake on the middle shelf of the oven for 30 minutes. • Arrange the baked apples in dessert bowls. When serving, warm the Calvados in a ladle over a candle at the table, ignite and sprinkle over the baked apples.

Our Tip: Instead of setting light to the apples, they may be served with a zabaglione sauce.

Apricot Dessert with Cracked Wheat
top right

500g/1lb 2oz fresh apricots	
80g/3½ oz cracked wheat	
100g/4oz coarsely chopped almonds	
100g/4oz honey	
250ml/8 fl oz single cream	
½ tsp vanilla essence	

Preparation time: 30 minutes
Nutritional value:
Analysis per serving, approx:
• 2400kJ/570kcal
• 10g protein
• 34g fat
• 55g carbohydrate

Wash the apricots in lukewarm water, dry well, halve and stone them. Cut the apricot halves into quarters. • Roast the cracked wheat and almonds in a heavy based, dry frying pan over a medium heat, turning constantly, until they darken and have a pleasant smell. • Add the prepared apricots and the honey and continue heating while stirring until the honey begins to caramelise. • Mix the cream and vanilla into the wheat and simmer, stirring, for another minute. • Transfer the dessert to a heated serving dish and serve while warm.

Our Tip: As an alternative to apricots, the dessert can be prepared with peaches, nectarines or plums.

Tarte Tatin

This caramelised apple tart is a classic French dessert

Ingredients for one 24-cm/10-inch tart:

1kg/2¼lbs eating apples (russet or Cox's orange pippin)
2 tbsps lemon juice
4 tbsps sugar
50g/2oz butter
200g/7oz flour
100g/4oz butter
1 tbsp icing sugar
1 egg yolk
Pinch of salt

Preparation time: 1 hour
Baking: 20 minutes
Nutritional value:
Analysis per serving (serves 8):
• 1600kJ/380kcal
• 5g protein
• 20g fat
• 41g carbohydrate

Peel the apples. Halve small apples and quarter larger ones, remove the cores and sprinkle with lemon juice. • Sprinkle a heavy-based flan dish or frying pan with sugar and dot with the 2oz of butter. Arrange the apples in the bottom of the flan dish. • Melt the butter in the dish over a low heat. Increase the heat, caramelise the butter and simmer gently. • Press the apples down slightly as they soften. As soon as the apples soften, the juice will run off into the caramel. At this point, remove the dish from the heat and allow the apples to cool. • Make a dough by mixing the 4 oz butter with the flour, icing sugar, egg yolk, salt and 5 tbsps water. • Heat the oven to 250°C/500°F/Gas Mark 9. • Roll out the pastry to form a 3mm/¼-inch thick circle 28cm/11 inches in diameter. Lay the pastry over the apples, pressing down round the apple shapes at the edges. • Bake the tart to a golden-brown on the middle shelf for 20 minutes. Turn off the oven and leave to rest for a further 10 minutes. • Turn out the tart onto a plate and serve warm with crème fraîche or whipped cream.

Kiwi Cheese Soufflé

Full of protein and vitamins, light and easy to digest

Stuffed Peaches

A delight for eyes and taste-buds

Ingredients for a 24-cm/10-inch pie:
2 eggs
250g/8oz quark or curd cheese
100ml/3 fl oz cream
3 tbsps kiwi liqueur or Grand Marnier (orange liqueur)
Pinch of salt
2 tbsps sugar
4 kiwi fruits
1 tbsp butter and 4 tbsps ground almonds for the dish
2 tbsps sifted icing sugar for dusting

Preparation time: 45 minutes
Baking: 15 minutes
Nutritional value:
Analysis per serving (serves 6):
• 1070kJ/260kcal
• 12g protein
• 12g fat
• 16g carbohydrate

Heat the oven to 220°C/425°F/Gas Mark 7.

Butter the dish and sprinkle with ground almonds. • Separate the egg whites from the yolks. • Mix the quark and the cream until smooth, then mix in the egg yolks and liqueur. • Whisk the egg whites and the salt until soft peaks form, gradually add the sugar and continue whisking until the egg whites are glossy. Fold the egg whites into the quark mixture. • Peel the kiwi fruits and cut into slices about 1/2cm/1/4-inch thick. • Place the quark cream in the dish and arrange the kiwi slices on it in a fan shape. • Bake on the middle shelf of the oven for 15 minutes until golden. • Dust with icing sugar and serve immediately.

Our Tip: This dessert can be made using other exotic fruits such as papayas or mangoes. Always try to find a liqueur that matches the taste of the fruit.

4 large peaches
125 ml/4 fl oz water
100g/4oz sugar
1/2 a lemon
3 egg whites
Pinch of ground cinnamon
4 tbsps redcurrant jelly or raspberry jam
50g/2oz chopped almonds

Preparation time: 15 minutes
Baking: 10 minutes
Nutritional value:
Analysis per serving, approx:
• 1300kJ/310kcal
• 12g protein
• 8g fat
• 50g carbohydrate

Heat the oven to 240°C/475°F/Gas Mark 9. Line a baking tin with baking parchment. • Prick the peaches with a fork several times, immerse briefly in boiling water and remove the skins; cut in half and remove the stones. • Mix 50g/2oz sugar with the water. Squeeze the lemon and add the juice to the water. Add the peaches and stew, covered, for 7 minutes on a low heat. • Whisk the egg whites until stiff, pour the remaining sugar and cinnamon into them and beat well for a further 2 minutes. • Mix the jelly or jam and chopped almonds and spoon into the drained peach halves. • Place the peaches on the baking sheet, spoon some whipped egg white over them and form small peaks. • Bake the peaches on the top shelf for 10 minutes. Serve immediately.

Banana Kisses

The meringue can be prepared in advance

Banana Fritters

Easy to prepare and especially delicious

125g/5oz icing sugar
2 egg whites
1 tsp lemon juice
2 bananas
15g/½ oz butter
2 tbsps chocolate vermicelli
Baking parchment and oil for the baking sheet

Preparation time: 40 minutes
Baking time: 2 hours
Nutritional value:
Analysis per serving, approx:
- 1200kJ/290kcal
- 7g protein
- 6g fat
- 51g carbohydrate

Heat the oven to 100°C/200°F/Gas Mark ¼. Lightly oil a baking sheet and line it with baking parchment. • Sift the icing sugar onto a piece of greaseproof paper. • Whisk the egg whites and lemon juice until stiff, gradually add the icing sugar, and continue whisking until the egg whites are shiny. • Place the egg whites in a piping bag with a plain nozzle and pipe four banana-shaped strips onto the baking paper. • Place the meringues on the middle shelf of the oven for two hours, keeping the oven door ajar with the handle of a wooden spoon; this dries out the meringue as opposed to baking it. • Peel the bananas and cut in half lengthways. • Melt the butter in a pan and gently fry the bananas on both sides until they begin to caramelise. • Arrange the bananas on the meringues and sprinkle with chocolate strands.

150g/5½oz flour
6 tbsps dry white wine
6 tbsps water
1 tbsp safflower oil
2 egg whites
Pinch of salt
4 medium bananas
2 tsps lemon juice
2 tsps icing sugar
2 tbsps sugar
1 tsp ground cinnamon
1l/1¾ pints safflower oil for deep frying

Preparation time: 1½ hours
Nutritional value:
Analysis per serving, approx:
- 1700kJ/400kcal
- 11g protein
- 8g fat
- 70g carbohydrate

Mix the wine, water and oil into the flour in a bowl to make a batter. • Whisk the egg whites with the salt until stiff and fold into the batter. Leave to rest for 30 minutes. • Heat the oil to 170°C/325°F in a deep fryer or saucepan using a sugar thermometer to check the temperature. Turn on the oven to its lowest setting. • Halve the bananas lengthways and slice into two crossways. Sprinkle the lemon juice over the bananas and sift the icing sugar over them. • Use a fork to dip the bananas in the batter and fry two or three pieces at a time for 3 minutes until golden. • Drain on absorbent paper and keep warm in the oven until all the bananas have been deep fried. • Mix the sugar and cinnamon together and sprinkle over the bananas.

Austrian Quark Soufflé

A princely finale to a festive meal

Ingredients for 6 individual soufflé dishes:

FOR THE APRICOT SAUCE:

500g/1lb 2oz ripe apricots
250ml/8 fl oz dry white wine
½ cinnamon stick
2 cloves

FOR THE SOUFFLÉS:

4 eggs
100g/4oz sugar
Pinch of salt
200g/7oz quark or low fat curd cheese
1 vanilla pod
2 tbsps rum
Grated rind of ½ a lemon
1 tbsp icing sugar to dust
Butter for the soufflé dishes

Preparation time: 40 minutes
Baking: 20 – 30 minutes
Nutritional value:
Analysis per serving, approx:
- 1400kJ/330kcal
- 14g protein
- 12g fat
- 32g carbohydrate

Wash, dry, halve and stone the apricots. Stew gently in the wine, cinnamon and cloves for 10 minutes and then purée in a mixer. • Cover the apricot sauce and reserve it. • Separate the eggs. Beat the egg yolks and sugar until fluffy. Whisk the egg whites with the salt until stiff. • Add the quark to the egg yolks. • Split the vanilla pod and scrape out the vanilla; mix with the rum, lemon rind and quark, and stir into the egg yolks. • Heat the oven to 180°C/350°F/Gas Mark 4. Butter the dishes. • Fold the egg whites into the quark mixture. Divide this between the dishes and stand them in a baking dish filled with hot water. Bake on the middle shelf of the oven for 20 to 30 minutes or until the soufflés are golden. • Dust with icing sugar and serve immediately with the apricot sauce.

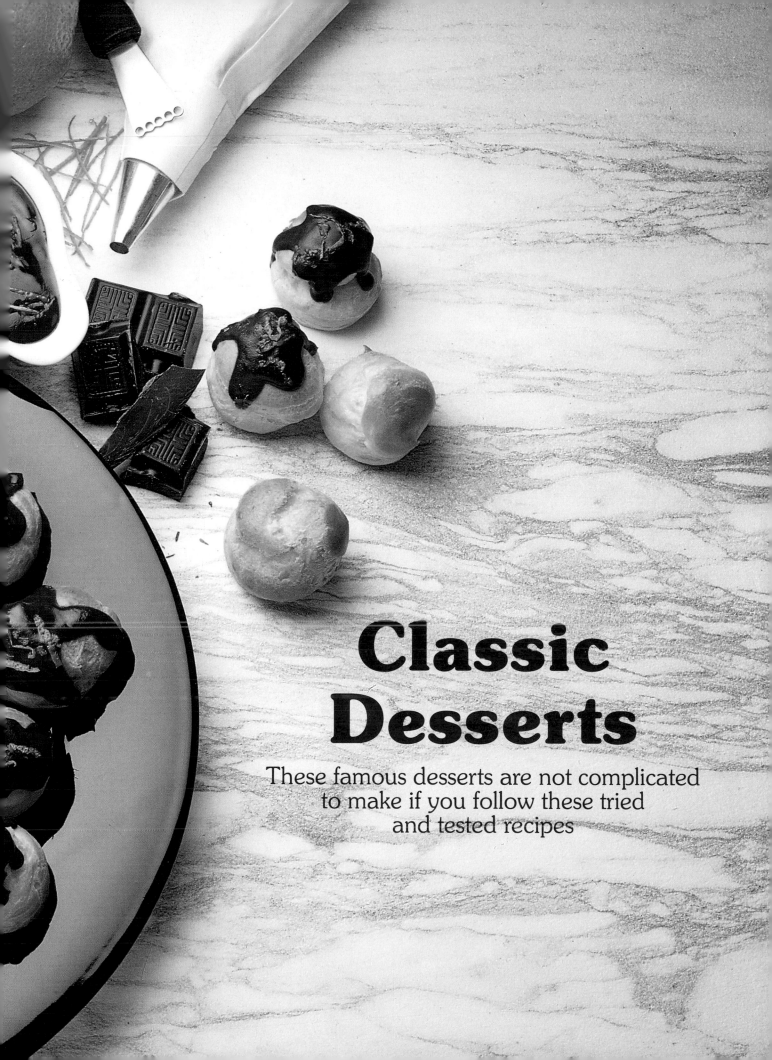

Classic Desserts

These famous desserts are not complicated
to make if you follow these tried
and tested recipes

A Dessert for the Cooler Season

These jellycreams can easily be prepared ahead of time and kept in the refrigerator until served

Orange Cream
top left

4 leaves gelatine or 2 tsps powdered gelatine
350ml/4 fl oz water
500g/1lb 2oz juicy oranges
4 egg yolks
50g/2oz sugar
1 tbsp vanilla sugar
2 tbsps Cointreau
2 egg whites
125ml/4 fl oz whipping cream

Preparation time: 30 minutes
Nutritional value:
Analysis per serving, approx:
• 1300kJ/310kcal
• 18g protein
• 22g fat
• 32g carbohydrate

Soak the leaf gelatine in the cold water. • Wash one orange in warm water, dry it and grate the rind. Reserve in the refrigerator. Squeeze the juice from all the oranges. • Beat the egg yolks with the sugar and vanilla sugar until fluffy. • Heat the orange juice. Press the liquid from the leaf gelatine and dissolve the gelatine in the hot orange juice (if using powdered gelatine, follow directions on packet). Combine this with the Cointreau and stir into the egg yolk mixture with the orange rind. • Place in the refrigerator. • Whisk the egg whites until stiff. Whip the cream until stiff. • Place two tbsps whipped cream in a piping-bag and fold the rest of the cream and the egg whites into the orange cream. Arrange in individual dessert bowls or glasses. • Peel half an orange very thinly and cut the rind into very fine julienne strips. Decorate the pudding with rosettes of cream and the reserved grated orange rind. Sprinkle with julienned orange.

Mocha Cream
top right

2 eggs • 1 tsp cocoa powder
500ml/16 fl oz milk
6 leaves gelatine or 1 tsp powdered gelatine
250ml/8 fl oz water
4 tbsps sugar • 1 tbsp vanilla sugar
5 tsps instant coffee powder
250ml/8 fl oz whipping cream
50g/2oz chocolate-flavoured coffee beans

Preparation time: 40 minutes
Chilling time: 1 hour
Nutritional value:
Analysis per serving, approx:
• 2010kJ/480kcal
• 16g protein
• 34g fat
• 28g carbohydrate

Separate the eggs. • Blend the egg yolks with the cocoa powder and four tbsps milk until smooth. • Soak the gelatine in the cold water. • Bring 250ml/8 fl oz milk to the boil with the sugar, vanilla sugar and coffee powder, stirring constantly. When it boils, remove from the heat. • Whisk the egg yolk mixture into the mocha milk. Press the liquid from the gelatine and dissolve the gelatine in the mocha milk, or combine 125ml/4 fl oz of the mocha milk with the powdered gelatine then mix well with the rest of the mocha milk • Refrigerate the mixture. • Whip the cream until stiff and chill it. • Whisk the egg whites until stiff and fold into the mocha milk once it begins to thicken. • Take two-thirds of the whipped cream, add to the setting mixture and stir it in with a spoon in swirls so that a marbled pattern results. • Place the mixture in dessert glasses and leave to set firmly in the refrigerator. • Decorate with the remaining whipped cream and chocolate-flavoured coffee beans.

Charlotte Royal

This dessert "fit for royalty" was invented 200 years ago and named after Queen Charlotte, wife of King George III

Ingredients for 12 portions:

FOR THE SWISS ROLL MIXTURE:

6 egg yolks

100g/4oz sugar

1 tbsp vanilla sugar

4 egg whites

Pinch of salt

100g/4oz flour

25g/1oz cornflour

FOR SPREADING:

480g/1lb 2oz raspberry jam

2 tbsps raspberry liqueur

For the cream:

7 leaves gelatine or 1 packet powdered gelatine

500ml/16 fl oz water

4 egg yolks

100g/4oz sugar

1/2 vanilla pod

Juice of 1 orange and 1 lemon

250ml/8 fl oz dry white wine

2 egg whites

Pinch of salt

250ml/8 fl oz cream

Extra sugar for sprinkling

Preparation time: 1¼ hours

Chilling time: 5 hours

Nutritional value:

Analysis per serving, approx:

- 1590kJ/380kcal
- 9g protein
- 12g fat
- 55g carbohydrate

Heat the oven to 220°C/425°F/Gas Mark 7. Use an electric beater to beat the egg yolks with 50g/2oz sugar and the vanilla sugar until the sugar has dissolved completely. Sift the flour and cornflour over the mixture and fold them in. • Whisk the egg whites with the salt until fluffy, then add the rest of the sugar and continue beating until stiff and glossy. Line a Swiss roll tin with baking parchment. • Fold the egg whites into the egg yolk mixture. • Spread the Swiss roll mixture on the baking sheet and bake for about 12 minutes on the upper shelf of the oven until golden. • Sprinkle a kitchen towel

with sugar, turn the Swiss roll onto the cloth, pull off the paper and cover the sponge with a damp cloth. • Stir the jam and the raspberry liqueur over a low heat until smooth, pass through a sieve and spread over the sponge. • Use the cloth to roll up the Swiss roll and leave to cool under the damp cloth. Now make the cream. • Soak leaf gelatine in the cold water. • Whisk the egg yolks with the sugar until fluffy. Split the vanilla pod lengthways, scrape out the inside and stir into the egg yolk mixture. • Strain the fruit juice and heat it. • Press the liquid from the leaf gelatine and dissolve in the warm juice (if using powdered gelatine, follow directions on packet). • Stir the wine into the egg yolk mixture and gradually whisk in the gelatine mixture. Place the mixture in the refrigerator. • Whisk the egg whites with the salt until stiff. Whip the cream until stiff. • As soon as the egg yolk mixture begins to

thicken, whisk the egg whites and whipped cream into the mixture and return to the refrigerator. • Cut the Swiss roll into 1cm/½-inch-thick slices and use them to line a bowl. Fill the mould with the cream mixture. • Leave to chill for at least five hours. • To serve, unmould onto a serving dish and cut into 12 equal slices like a gateau.

Our Tip: You can use the leftover egg whites to make meringues: whisk the egg whites with 200g/7oz caster or icing sugar and 3 tsps cornflour until stiff and pipe or spoon onto a baking tray lined with baking parchment. Dry rather than bake for two hours at 100°C/200°F/Gas Mark ¼ in the oven, leaving the oven door ajar. Remove the meringues from the oven, leave to cool completely and store in an airtight tin.

Creamy Desserts for Gourmets

These old-fashioned desserts deserve a revival

Tea Cream
top left

Ingredients for four 200ml/6 fl oz ramekins:

8 tsps black tea leaves
100ml/3 fl oz boiling water
100g/4oz brown lump sugar
500ml/16 fl oz cream
3 egg yolks
1 tsp lemon juice
FOR THE RAMEKINS:
Oil for greasing
4 tsps raw cane sugar

Preparation time: 30 minutes
Cooking time: 25 minutes
Chilling time: 2 hours
Nutritional value:
Analysis per serving, approx:
• 2310kJ/550kcal
• 15g protein
• 64g fat
• 34g carbohydrate

Warm a teapot, place the tea leaves in it, pour on the boiling water and leave to infuse for two minutes. Strain the tea and mix with the lump sugar. • Take 125ml/4 fl oz cream and place in the refrigerator. Bring the remainder of the cream to the boil, stirring, allow to thicken slightly, remove from the heat and gradually whisk in the egg yolks. Gradually pour in the tea. Continue to whisk the mixture over a low heat until it thickens. • Heat the oven to 160°C/310°F/Gas Mark 2-3. Fill a large, shallow pan with boiling water and put the ramekins in it. Brush the the ramekins with oil and sprinkle with the sugar. • Divide the mixture between the ramekins and allow to set on the bottom shelf of the oven for 25 minutes. • Leave to cool and then chill in the refrigerator. Beat the remaining cream until stiff, mix with the lemon juice and pour onto the cream before serving.

Russian Cream
top right

4 leaves gelatine or 2 tsps powdered
125ml/4 fl oz water
6 egg yolks
150g/5¹/₂oz icing sugar
1¹/₂ tsps grated orange rind
125ml/4 fl oz dry white wine
2 tbsps vodka
2 tbsps orange juice
200m/6 fl oz whipping cream

Preparation time: 45 minutes
Chilling time: 2 hours
Nutritional value:
Analysis per serving, approx:
• 1760kJ/420kcal
• 26g protein
• 64g fat
• 42g carbohydrate

Soak the leaf gelatine in the cold water. • Beat the egg yolks in a bowl, sift on the icing sugar with ¹/₂ tsp orange rind and beat until fluffy. Slowly stir in the white wine and vodka and continue beating for several minutes. • Heat the orange juice. Squeeze the leaf gelatine and dissolve, stirring, in the hot juice (if using powdered, follow directions on packet). Stir the gelatine into the egg yolk mixture and place in the refrigerator. • Whip the cream until stiff. As soon as the egg yolk mixture begins to thicken, fold in the whipped cream, transfer to individual serving bowls or glasses, then cover and leave in the refrigerator to cool and set. • Sprinkle the rest of the orange rind over the Russian Cream before serving.

Paskha

This traditional Russian Easter dessert is prepared a day in advance

Ingredients for a 1500ml/2¹/₂-pint pudding bowl:

1kg/2¹/₄lbs quark or other low-fat cheese
200g/7oz mixed candied fruits
25g/1oz candied orange peel
25g/1oz candied lemon peel
50g/2oz ground almonds
1 tsp ground vanilla
175g/6oz soft butter
200ml/6 fl oz cream
3 egg yolks
175g/6oz sugar
50g/2oz blanched almonds

Preparation time: 1¹/₂ hours
Resting time: 12 hours
Nutritional value:
Analysis per serving (serves 8):
• 2800kJ/670kcal
• 26g protein
• 59g fat
• 50g carbohydrate

Empty the quark into a sieve lined with a muslin cloth. Place the sieve over a bowl, fold the muslin over the top of the quark and weight it down to squeeze out the liquid. • Dice 100g/4oz candied fruits as well as the candied orange and lemon peel and mix with the almonds and vanilla. • Strain the quark through the sieve, having removed the muslin cloth. Beat the butter until fluffy and mix into the quark. • Warm up the cream. Mix the egg yolks and sugar in a high saucepan until creamy and slowly stir in the cream, heating the mixture while stirring, but not allowing it to boil. Place the saucepan in a bowl of water with ice cubes and allow the mixture to cool. • Stir in the fruit mixture and spoonfuls of quark. • Line the pudding bowl with a damp muslin cloth, leaving the edges overhanging the sides, and fill with the mixture. Wrap the ends of the cloth over the pudding and weight the mixture. Refrigerate for 12 hours. • Turn out the Paskha and remove the cloth. • Lightly toast the almonds. Decorate the Paskha with the almonds and the rest of the candied fruit.

Crème Caramel

The classic baked egg custard which will keep in the refrigerator for 24 hours or more

Ingredients for 8 ovenproof pudding moulds:

150g/5½oz sugar
500ml/16 fl oz milk
1 tsp vanilla essence
4 eggs
4 egg yolks
Melted butter for the moulds

Preparation time: 30 minutes
Cooking time: 40-50 minutes
Chilling time: 3 hours
Nutritional value:
Analysis per serving, approx:
• 840kJ/200kcal
• 13g protein
• 21g fat
• 18g carbohydrate

Brush the moulds with butter. • Boil 100g/4oz sugar with five tbsps water, stirring constantly, until the steam ceases to rise and the sugar has caramelised to a golden yellow. Spoon the caramel immediately into the moulds and rock them to and fro to coat completely with caramel. • Heat the milk and vanilla. Mix the eggs, egg yolks and remaining sugar, but do not beat. Slowly whisk the hot vanilla milk into the egg mixture. • Heat the oven to 175°C/335°F/Gas Mark 3-4. Fill a baking dish with enough water to reach half way up the moulds. • Pour the egg milk into the moulds, place them in the baking dish and allow the custard to set on the middle shelf for 40 minutes. • Gently test with a finger whether the crème has set sufficiently and leave for a few minutes more if necessary. • Allow the crème to cool slightly in the moulds and refrigerate for at least three hours. • Shortly before serving, loosen the edges with a sharp knife and turn out the crème caramel on plates.

Classic Mousses and Jelly Creams

Whether coffee or chocolate, these desserts are always popular

Mousse au Chocolat
top left

Ingredients for 8 portions:
100g/4oz dark bitter chocolate

100g/4oz plain chocolate

100g/4oz butter

6 eggs

2 tsps grated orange rind

3 tbsps Grand Marnier (orange liqueur)

Pinch of salt

2 tbsps icing sugar

125ml/4 fl oz whipping cream

Preparation time: 1 hour
Chilling time: 5 hours
Nutritional value:
Analysis per serving, approx:
• 1470kJ/350kcal
• 11g protein
• 31g fat
• 17g carbohydrate

Break the chocolate into pieces and melt with 1 tbsp water over a pan of simmering water. Add knobs of butter and continue stirring until completely smooth. Keep the chocolate mixture warm over the simmering water. • Separate the eggs. Stir the egg yolks with 1 tbsp water over the pan of simmering water until creamy. Add the orange rind, liqueur and chocolate mixture to the egg yolks. • Whisk the egg whites with the salt until stiff. • Sift the icing powder into the cream, beat until stiff and fold, with the egg whites, into the chocolate mixture. • Leave for about five hours in the refrigerator to set.

Coffee Cream with Cherries
top right

3 tsps instant coffee powder

400g/14oz fresh cherries

2 tbsps sugar

5 tbsps white wine or unsweetened grape juice

2 eggs

Pinch of salt

3 tbsps icing sugar

250ml/8 fl oz whipping cream

Preparation time: 30 minutes
Chilling time: 1 hour
Nutritional value:
Analysis per serving, approx:
• 1680kJ/400kcal
• 9g protein
• 26g fat
• 29g carbohydrate

Dissolve the coffee powder in 1 tbsp boiling water and allow to cool. • Wash and stone the cherries. • Mix the sugar with the wine or grape juice, pour over the cherries, then cover and stew over a low heat for five to seven minutes. • Drain the cherries in a sieve, reserve the juice and place both in the refrigerator. • Separate the eggs. Whisk the egg whites with the salt until stiff. Whisk the egg yolks with the icing sugar until fluffy and gradually add the cold cherry juice. • Arrange the cherries in among four dessert glasses. Whip the cream until stiff and mix with the coffee. • Fold the egg whites and whipped cream into the egg yolk mixture. Spread the coffee cream over the cherries and serve at once.

Variations on Mousse au Chocolat

Mousse in any form is a delicious temptation

Mousse au Chocolat Blanc
top left

Ingredients for 6 portions:
200g/7oz white chocolate
2 tbsps raspberry liqueur
100g/4oz crème fraîche
2 egg whites
Pinch of salt
2 tbsps vanilla sugar
125ml/4 fl oz whipping cream
500g/1lb 2oz raspberries
2 tbsps icing sugar
12 mint leaves to decorate

Preparation time: 40 minutes
Chilling time: 2 hours
Nutritional value:
Analysis per serving, approx:
• 1680kJ/400kcal
• 8g protein
• 25g fat
• 34g carbohydrate

Break the chocolate into small pieces, mix with the raspberry liqueur and stir to melt over a pan of simmering water. Stir in the crème fraîche. • Whisk the egg whites and salt until fluffy, slowly pour in the vanilla sugar and whisk until stiff. Also whip the cream until stiff. • Fold the egg whites and whipped cream into the white chocolate cream, put in a bowl and refrigerate for two hours until set. •Wash, clean and drain the raspberries, then strain them through a sieve. Mix the raspberry purée and icing sugar. Wash and pat dry the mint leaves. • Before serving, make pools of raspberry purée on serving plates. Dip a spoon in cold water and spoon knobs of mousse onto the fruit purée. Decorate with mint leaves.

Marbled Mousse
top right

Ingredients for 6 portions:
150g/5¹/₂oz each plain and white chocolate
3 eggs
250ml/8 fl oz cream
2 tbsps caster sugar
3 tbsps espresso or strong coffee
3 tbsps white rum
Icing sugar

Preparation time: 45 minutes
Chilling time: 2 hours
Nutritional value:
Analysis per serving, approx:
• 2100kJ/500kcal
• 10g protein
• 34g fat
• 34g carbohydrate

Break both sorts of chocolate into pieces and melt, each with 1 tbsp water, over a pan of simmering water. • Separate the eggs. Whisk the egg whites until stiff. • Whip the cream. • Dissolve the sugar with two tbsps hot water until dissolved. Beat gradually into the egg yolks until the mixture is fluffy. • Divide the egg yolk mixture. Gradually add the plain chocolate and espresso to one half; likewise add the white chocolate and rum to the other half. • Divide the egg whites and whipped cream and whisk both into each cream mixture. • Put the dark mousse in a bowl, place the white mousse on top and mix both in spiral motion with a fork. • Leave for two hours to set. • Sift icing sugar over six dessert plates. Spoon knobs of mousse onto the dessert plates using a dessert spoon dipped in cold water.

Pears with Chocolate Sauce

A classic taste combination

150g/5½oz blanched almonds
75g/3oz honey
2 tbsps rosewater
100g/4oz honey-sweetened chocolate (health food shop)
2 ripe pears
1 egg white
100ml/4 fl oz whipping cream

Preparation time: 40 minutes
Nutritional value:
Analysis per serving, approx:
- 2350kJ/560kcal
- 12g protein
- 36g fat
- 47g carbohydrate

Grind the almonds very finely or use a mixer. • Mix the almonds and the honey, placing the bowl in a saucepan of hot water and stirring until the honey and almonds have formed a smooth mixture. Mix the rosewater into the almond and honey marzipan. • Break the chocolate into pieces and melt in a small saucepan on an extremely low heat or stand in a pan of simmering water. • Wash the pears in warm water, dry them, cut in half, removing the cores, and arrange each pear on a dessert plate, cut surface down. • Whisk the egg white until stiff and fold into the marzipan. • Whip the cream until stiff and place in a piping bag with a star nozzle. • Cover the pear halves in marzipan. Drizzle the chocolate sauce over the pears and decorate with blobs of cream.

Maple Cream with Walnuts

A special dessert, especially popular with children

2 leaves of gelatine, or 1 tsp powdered
125ml/4 fl oz water (omit if using powdered gelatin)
50g/2oz brown rice-flour
Pinch of ground vanilla
10 tbsps maple syrup
100g/4oz shelled walnuts
100g/4oz crème fraîche
2 tbsps lemon juice
200ml/6 fl oz cream

Preparation time: 30 minutes
Chilling time: 1 hour
Nutritional value:
Analysis per serving, approx:
- 2300kJ/550kcal
- 8g protein
- 44g fat
- 33g carbohydrate

Soak the leaf gelatine in cold water. • Mix the rice flour and vanilla and stir till smooth with 100ml/3 fl oz water. Bring 250ml/8 fl oz water to the boil, pour in the rice flour mixture, stirring, and gently boil for not quite three minutes. • Remove the saucepan from the heat and stir in two tbsps maple syrup. • Set aside four walnut pieces. Chop the rest coarsely and toast gently in a dry pan stirring all the time. Add four tbsps maple syrup and allow to caramelise slightly over a medium heat. Stir the hot nuts into the rice mixture. • Press the liquid from the gelatine and stir into the hot rice mixture until dissolved (if using powdered, follow directions on packet). Add the crème fraîche and lemon juice also. • Whip the cream until stiff, fold into the cooling mixture and place in the refrigerator to chill. • Arrange the maple cream in dessert bowls, decorate with a walnut and a tbsp maple syrup. Should not be served too chilled.

Delicacies for Midsummer

Buy only ripe fruit that smells sweet

Gooseberry Trifle
top left

Ingredients for 6 portions:

500g/1lb 2oz gooseberries
125ml/4 fl oz water
150g/5½oz raw cane sugar
4 eggs
500ml/16 fl oz milk
4 sponge fingers
100ml/3 fl oz Madeira
12 almond macaroons
5 candied pineapple rings
5 slices of orange
125ml/4 fl oz cream
2 tsps vanilla sugar

Preparation time: 1 hour
Chilling time: 4 hours
Nutritional value:

Analysis per serving, approx:
- 2400kJ/520kcal
- 14g protein
- 33g fat
- 81g carbohydrate

Clean and top and tail the gooseberries. Cook gently, covered, in the water with 100g/4oz raw cane sugar for 10 minutes; then allow to cool. • Whisk the eggs with the rest of the granulated sugar until fluffy. Heat the milk and slowly add to the egg mixture, stirring continuously, and heat gently on a very low heat, stirring until the cream has thickened. Do not allow to boil. • Place the pan in a bowl with ice cubes and stir until cool. • Line a glass bowl with the sponge fingers and sprinkle with Madeira. Cover with the gooseberries, then add the almond macaroons and soak them with Madeira as well. • Pour the creamy mixture over the macaroons. Leave the dessert for four hours in the refrigerator to steep and set. • Finely dice the candied fruit. Whip the cream with the vanilla sugar until stiff, spread over the dessert and decorate with the fruit. This may also be served in individual bowls.

Melon Chandeau
top right

1 medium-sized honeydew melon,
8 leaves of gelatine or 1 packet powdered
500ml/16 fl oz water (omit if using powdered)
5 eggs
150g/5½oz sugar
125ml/4 fl oz dry white wine
1 tbsp lemon juice
Pinch of salt
Sprig of mint
125ml/4 fl oz whipping cream

Preparation time: 1 hour
Setting time: 4 hours
Nutritional value:

Analysis per serving, approx:
- 1630kJ/390kcal
- 22g protein
- 24g fat
- 50g carbohydrate

Halve the melon and remove the pips. Remove the flesh from one half of the melon using a melon baller; cover and set aside. Remove the flesh from the other half • Soak the leaf gelatine in the water. • Separate three eggs. Whisk the yolks with the whole eggs and sugar over a pan of simmering water until fluffy. • Slowly add the wine and lemon juice and continue stirring until the mixture thickens. Remove from the heat but keep warm over the hot water. • Press the liquid from the gelatine and dissolve it in the warm mixture (if using powdered, follow directions on packet). • Purée the melon flesh, stir into the mixture, strain through a fine sieve and leave to cool. • Whisk the egg whites with the salt until stiff. As soon as the mixture begins to thicken, fold in the egg whites and melon balls. • Set in the refrigerator. • Decorate with the mint. • Whip the cream into soft peaks and serve with the dessert.

The Moor in a Shirt

A classic dessert from central Europe

Ingredients for a 1.5l/2½-pint pudding mould:
80g/3oz wholemeal semolina
20g/¾oz cocoa powder
70g/3oz raw cane sugar
Grated rind of 1 orange
2 tsps vanilla essence
250ml/8 fl oz milk
50g/2oz butter, melted
100g/4oz honey
100g/4oz blanched ground almonds
4 eggs
200ml/6 fl oz whipping cream
Butter and wholemeal breadcrumbs for the dish

Preparation time: 40 minutes
Cooking time: 2 hours
Nutritional value:
Analysis per serving (serves 8):
• 1800kJ/430kcal
• 12g protein
• 28g fat
• 31g carbohydrate

Mix the semolina with the cocoa, a third of the sugar, the orange rind and some vanilla. • Bring the milk to the boil, stir in the semolina and boil for two minutes. • Take the saucepan off the heat, add the butter, honey and almonds and leave to cool. • Brush a pudding mould with butter and sprinkle with breadcrumbs. • Separate the eggs. Stir the yolks into the semolina. • Whisk the egg whites until stiff, then gradually add a third of the sugar and continue beating until stiff. Fold into the semolina and pour the mixture into the mould, cover tightly and place in a saucepan of boiling water to cook for one hour. • Whip the cream with the remaining sugar and the rest of the vanilla until it forms soft peaks. Allow the pudding to cool slightly and then turn out on a serving dish and pour over the vanilla cream.

Zuppa Romana

Alchermes is a herbal liqueur from Florence. Sherry may be substituted

FOR THE SPONGE:
3 eggs
80g/3oz sugar
1 tbsp vanilla sugar
Pinch of salt
50g/2oz flour
30g/1oz cornflour
FOR THE FILLING:
500ml/16 fl oz milk
1 tbsp vanilla sugar
5 eggs
120g/5oz sugar
30g/1oz flour
150g/5½oz candied fruits
3 tbsps Alchermes or sherry
100g/4oz icing sugar

Preparation time: 2 hours
Chilling time: 3 hours
Nutritional value:
Analysis per serving (serves 8):
• 2010kJ/480kcal
• 16g protein
• 27g fat
• 67g carbohydrate

Heat the oven to 180°C/350°F/Gas Mark 4. • Separate the eggs, beat the yolks with the sugars until fluffy, then fold in the flour and cornflour. Whisk the whites and salt until stiff and fold into the yolks. • Put the mixture in a cake tin and bake for 25 minutes until golden, then leave to cool. • Heat the milk and vanilla sugar. • Separate the eggs. Beat the yolks with the sugar and flour until fluffy, then slowly pour in the hot milk, stirring constantly. Bring to the boil and then cool. • Dice the fruit. • Cut the sponge into ½cm/¼-inch strips. • Heat the oven to 160°C/310°F/Gas Mark 2-3. • Line a gratin dish with strips of sponge and sprinkle with the liqueur. Add alternate layers of cream mixture and fruit. • Whisk the egg whites and icing sugar, spread onto the dessert and brown in the oven for 15 minutes. • Cool before serving.

Cinnamon Puddings on Armagnac Cream

A dessert for connoisseurs

Ingredients for 6 soufflé moulds or muffin tins:

125g/5oz stoned prunes
6 tbsps Armagnac
100g/4oz honey cake
3 tsps ground cinnamon
Pinch of ground cloves
50g/2oz chocolate flakes
4 eggs
100g/4oz soft butter
2 tbsps icing sugar
Pinch of salt
50g/2oz finely chopped walnuts
100g/4oz crème fraîche
6 mint leaves
Butter and sugar for the moulds

Soaking time: 12 hours
Preparation time: 1 hour
Baking time: 20 minutes
Nutritional value:
Analysis per serving, approx:
• 2310kJ/550kcal
• 11g protein
• 38g fat
• 39g carbohydrate

Soak the prunes in the Armagnac for 12 hours. • Grind the honey cake finely in a food processor or liquidizer, then mix in the cinnamon, ground cloves and chocolate flakes. • Separate the egg whites from the yolks. • Cream the butter and icing sugar and add egg yolks, one by one. • Whisk the egg whites and salt until stiff, fold into the butter cream, sprinkle on the honey cake mixture and the nuts, and mix gently. • Heat the oven to 225°C/435°F/Gas Mark 7-8. Grease the moulds with butter and sprinkle with sugar. • Pour the mixture into the moulds and bake on the middle shelf of the oven for 17 to 20 minutes. • Turn the puddings onto six dessert plates and allow to cool. • Set aside six of the marinated prunes. Quickly purée the rest with the crème fraîche in the the food processor or liquidizer, adding white wine if necessary. Pour the sauce around the puddings and decorate with prunes and mint leaves.

Cream Bavaroise

This delicious dessert was created in the 14th century by the French Queen Isabella of Bavaria

Ingredients for 6 portions:

6 leaves of gelatine or 2¹/₂ tsps powdered
250ml/8 fl oz water (omit if using powdered)
1 vanilla pod
250ml/8 fl oz milk
5 egg yolks
100g/4oz sugar
250ml/8 fl oz whipping cream

Preparation time: 30 minutes
Setting time: 4 hours
Nutritional value:
Analysis per serving, approx:
• 1190kJ/280kcal
• 18g protein
• 41g fat
• 21g carbohydrate

Soak the leaf gelatine in the cold water. • Split the vanilla pod lengthwise and scrape out the inside. • Heat the empty pod in the milk and then leave to cool. • Use an electric beater to beat the egg yolks, vanilla and sugar over a pan of simmering water until thick and fluffy. • Remove the vanilla pod from the milk and pour it into the egg yolk mixture, continuing to beat over the hot water until the mixture is hot and thick. • Squeeze the liquid from the leaf gelatine and dissolve, stirring in a small saucepan over a pan of simmering water. Fold into the vanilla cream (if using powdered, follow directions on packet). • Put the mixture into the refrigerator. • Whip the cream until stiff and fold into the thickening mixture. • Place in four individual dishes which have been rinsed with cold water and refrigerate for four hours until it sets. • Turn out the Crème Bavaroise onto plates and decorate with lightly sugared berries, cold fruit sauces or rosettes of cream.

Our Tip: For a delicious chocolate dessert substitute 100g/4oz melted plain chocolate and two tsps each of instant coffee and cocoa powder for the vanilla. For almond cream, mix the egg yolks with 100g/4oz blanched and finely ground almonds, one tsp rosewater and two tsps Amaretto (almond liqueur).

Profiteroles

Originally the pride of French cuisine, now famous world-wide

Ingredients for 6 portions:

FOR THE BATTER:

125g/5oz flour

125ml/4 fl oz each of water and milk

50g/2oz butter

Pinch of salt

4 eggs

1 egg yolk

FOR THE VANILLA SAUCE:

½ vanilla pod

375ml/14 fl oz milk

40g/1½oz flour

3 egg yolks

75g/3oz sugar

1 tbsp butter

2 tbsps rum

FOR THE CHOCOLATE SAUCE:

100g/4oz plain chocolate

50g/2oz double cream

1 tbsp grated orange rind

Preparation time: 90 minutes
Baking time: 20 minutes

Nutritional value:

Analysis per serving, approx:
- 2310kJ/550kcal
- 25g protein
- 50g fat
- 46g carbohydrate

Heat the oven to 225°C/435°F/Gas Mark 7-8. Sift the flour onto greaseproof paper. Bring the water and the milk, butter and salt to the boil, pour in the flour all at once and stir until the dough forms a ball and separates from the bottom of the pan. Remove from the heat and, with a wooden spoon, vigorously beat in the eggs one by one. Set aside to cool. Line a baking sheet with baking parchment. • Fill a piping bag with the choux pastry and pipe walnut-sized balls onto the baking sheet through a plain nozzle. • Brush the choux with the egg yolk which has been thinned with 1 tsp water. Bake on the middle shelf of the oven for 20 minutes until golden brown. • Prick each choux on its side with a sharp knife to allow the steam to escape. Leave to cool. • To make the sauce, split the vanilla pod lengthwise, add it to the milk and bring to the boil. Turn off the heat and leave to stand for at least 10 minutes. • Mix the flour with the egg yolks and sugar. • Remove the vanilla pod from the milk and pour onto the egg yolk mixture. Return to the saucepan and, stirring constantly, bring back to the boil; remove from heat, cool slightly and pour into a bowl. • Melt the butter and brush the surface of the custard with it to prevent a skin from forming. Chill the mixture and stir in the rum when cold. • Put the cream into a piping bag with a very small nozzle. Push the nozzle from below into the profiteroles and fill them with the mixture (do not cut them). Arrange the profiteroles on a serving dish in a pyramid, or grouped. • Break the chocolate into pieces, add 3 tbsps water and melt over a pan of simmering water. • Mix the double cream and grated orange rind into the chocolate sauce. Pour the sauce over the profiteroles. If wished, sprinkle orange julienne strips over them.

Our Tip: Profiteroles – a fine choux pastry mixture – only taste good when freshly baked. Instead of orange rind you could add finely sliced, preserved ginger to the sauce for a fine aroma. Sometimes profiteroles are also decorated with very thin strands of caramel.

Trauttmansdorff Rice

A tasty dessert made with brown rice

100g/4oz short-grain brown rice
500ml/16 fl oz milk
1/2 tsp ground vanilla
Rind of 1/2 a lemon
50g/2 oz raw cane sugar
4 leaves of gelatine or 2 tsps powdered
250ml/8 fl oz water (omit if using powdered gelatine)
50g/2oz dried stoned apricots
30g/1oz crystallised ginger
1 ripe mango, about 300g/10oz
200ml/6 fl oz cream
1 tbsp lemon juice

Preparation time: 40 minutes
Cooking time: 1 1/4 hours
Setting time: 3 hours
Nutritional value:
Analysis per serving, approx:
• 2010kJ/480kcal
• 10g protein
• 26g fat
• 66g carbohydrate

Gently simmer the rice with the milk, vanilla, lemon rind and sugar for 40 minutes, then cover and allow to stand for 30 minutes. • Soak the leaf gelatine in the cold water. • Wash, dry and coarsely chop the apricots. Finely chop the ginger. Peel the mango thinly, slice the flesh from the stone and dice. • Remove lemon rind from the rice and mix in the apricot and ginger. • Press the liquid from the gelatine, stir into the hot rice and allow to dissolve (if using powdered, follow directions on packet). Lastly stir in the mango pieces. • Put the rice in the refrigerator until it begins to set. • Whip the cream with the rest of the sugar until stiff, mix in with the lemon juice and fold into the rice. Transfer the mixture to a mould which has been rinsed with cold water and leave in the refrigerator for three hours to set. • Turn out onto a serving dish and decorate with strips of dried apricot before serving.

Coconut Milk Jelly

A special dessert for festive occasions

125ml/4 fl oz milk
400ml/15 fl oz whipping cream
100g/4oz coconut flakes
4 leaves of gelatine or 2 tsps powdered
250ml/8 fl oz water (omit if using powdered)
4 egg yolks • 50g/2oz sugar
2 egg whites • 8 sponge fingers
6 tbsps orange liqueur
1 orange
2 tsps icing sugar

Preparation time: 1 1/4 hours
Chilling time: 2 hours
Nutritional value:
Analysis per serving, approx:
• 2930kJ/700kcal
• 23g protein
• 71g fat
• 32g carbohydrate

Bring the milk and half the cream to the boil; pour over the coconut flakes. Cover and leave for 30 minutes. • Soak the leaf gelatine in the cold water. •

Beat the egg yolks with the sugar until fluffy. • Squeeze the coconut flakes in a cloth over a bowl. Heat the coconut milk, mix with the egg yolks and stir over a pan of hot water until creamy. • Squeeze the gelatine, dissolve in the warm egg mixture and leave to cool (if using powdered, follow directions on packet). • Beat the egg whites and the remaining cream separately until stiff. • Once the coconut mixture begins to set, fold in the egg whites and whipped cream and place half the mixture in a bowl. • Soak the sponge fingers in the liqueur, place on the mixture, pour in the rest of the mixture and leave in the refrigerator for two hours. • Grate half the orange rind. • In a dry frying pan, toast 3 tbsps of coconut flakes with the icing sugar and orange rind until light brown. • Divide the orange into skinless segments. • Decorate the jelly with orange segments and coconut flakes.

Syllabub

Once Queen Victoria's favourite dessert

50g/2oz icing sugar
Grated rind of a lemon
8 tbsps dry or medium sherry
250ml/8 fl oz cream
1 tsp ground cinnamon

Preparation time: 10 minutes
Chilling time: 2 to 12 hours
Nutritional value:
Analysis per serving, approx:
- 1090kJ/260kcal
- 2g protein
- 20g fat
- 15g carbohydrate

Sift the icing sugar into a high mixing bowl. • Add half the lemon rind, the sherry, cream and cinnamon and beat with an electric beater until stiff peaks form. • Put the cream into dessert glasses and leave in the refrigerator for at least two, but preferably twelve, hours. • Reserve the rest of the lemon rind, wrapped in foil and as airtight as possible, in the refrigerator so that it does not dry out. • Sprinkle the rest of the lemon rind over the dessert just before serving.

Our Tip: As an alternative to sherry, syllabub can be prepared using white wine, port, Madeira or marsala. In the old days, syllabub was served first thing in the morning. However, it was not made with cream but with milk which had been milked straight into a vessel with some sherry.

Italian Dessert Hits

Some of the most popular desserts, and not only in Italy

Zabaglione
top left

4 tbsps icing sugar

4 egg yolks

12 tbsps dry marsala

Preparation time: 30 minutes
Nutritional value:
Analysis per serving, approx:
• 735kJ/175kcal
• 8g protein
• 10g fat
• 12g carbohydrate

Sift the icing sugar. • Heat some water in a shallow saucepan until just below boiling point. • Beat the egg yolks and icing sugar in a high-sided bowl, standing in the hot water, until fluffy. Gradually whisk in the marsala until the mixture thickens – alternatively, an electric beater may be used. • Transfer the cream to individual glass bowls while still warm and serve immediately. To serve cold, remove the bowl from the pan of hot water and continue beating until it is cool. • Serve small biscuits such as macaroons or brandy snaps with the dessert.

Our Tip: The water in the pan must not boil during the whole procedure. Have a glass of cold water next to the stove and regulate the temperature of the water by adding cold water when needed.

Tiramisu
top right

Ingredients for 8 portions:

150g/5¹/₂oz sponge fingers

125-250ml/4-8 fl oz espresso or strong coffee

4 egg yolks

100g/4oz icing sugar

2 tbsps Amaretto (Italian almond liqueur)

500g/1lb 2oz mascarpone (Italian curd cheese)

2 tbsps low-fat chocolate powder

Preparation time: 30 minutes
Chilling time: 3 hours
Nutritional value:
Analysis per serving, approx:
• 2180kJ/520kcal
• 18g protein
• 38g fat
• 26g carbohydrate

Arrange half the sponge fingers in the bottom of a square or rectangular dish and brush repeatedly with the coffee. The sponge should be well soaked but not mushy. • Beat the egg yolks with the icing sugar and Amaretto until fluffy; then gradually mix in the mascarpone. • Put mascarpone mixture onto the sponge, top with the remaining sponge fingers and brush them with coffee. • Distribute the rest of the cream over the sponge fingers and sift on chocolate powder. • Refrigerate Tiramisu for at least three hours before serving.

Our Tip: Instead of Amaretto flavour with two tsps vanilla essence. The dessert may be prepared in advance: leave it overnight in the refrigerator to allow the flavours to permeate the mixture.

Elegant Melon Desserts

Mouthwatering recipes that bring out the wonderful taste of melon

Melon with Peach Cream
top left

1 honeydew melon

4 tbsps medium sherry

500g/1lb 2oz ripe yellow peaches

2 tbsps lemon juice

½ vanilla pod

1 tbsp sugar

200ml/6 fl oz double cream

Preparation time: 20 minutes
Nutritional value:
Analysis per serving, approx:
• 1090kJ/260kcal
• 3g protein
• 16g fat
• 24g carbohydrate

Cut the melon in half, remove the pips, cut into wedges and sprinkle with sherry. • Prick the peaches with a fork several times, dip in boiling water, skin, halve, remove the stone, cut into pieces and purée in the food processor or liquidizer with the lemon juice, or strain through a fine sieve. • Split the vanilla pod lengthwise and scrape out the inside. Mix this and the sugar into the cream and stir until creamy. • Divide the fruit purée between four dessert plates, cover with cream and mix in with a wooden skewer in a spiral motion. • Arrange the marinated melon wedges beside it. • Serve at once.

Melon Bavaroise
top right

2 ogen or chanterais melons

50g/2oz sugar

125ml/4 fl oz dry sherry

4 leaves of gelatine or 2 tsps powdered

250ml/8 fl oz water (omit if using powdered)

½ vanilla pod

2 tbsps icing sugar

400ml/15 fl oz whipping cream

Preparation time: 40 minutes
Marination time: 1 hour
Setting time: 1 to 2 hours
Nutritional value:
Analysis per serving, approx:
• 1820kJ/435kcal
• 5g protein
• 32g fat
• 30g carbohydrate

Wash, dry and halve the melons; remove the pips. • Spoon out the flesh leaving only a 1cm/½-inch layer in the shell. Leave the melon halves to drain, cut side down. • Mix the sugar and sherry, pour over the melon flesh and leave, covered, for one hour to marinate. • Soak the leaf gelatine in the cold water. • Split the vanilla pod lengthwise, scrape out the inside and stir, with the icing sugar, into the cream. • Drain half the reserved melon flesh, dice and refrigerate. • Purée the remainder in a food processor or liquidiser with the marinade or push through a fine sieve. • Squeeze the water out of the gelatine, place in a metal container and dissolve over a pan of hot water (if using powdered, follow directions on packet); then spoon into the melon purée. • Whip the cream until stiff. Once the purée begins to thicken, mix in the cream and the melon cubes. Fill the melon halves with the purée and leave in the refrigerator to set.

Peach Tart on Nougat

This dish tastes best with ripe peaches

6 rusks • ½ tsp ground cinnamon

125g/5oz nut nougat

2 ripe peaches • ¼ vanilla pod

75g/3oz sugar

Juice and grated rind of lemon

125ml/4 fl oz sherry

3 leaves of gelatine or 1½ tsps powdered

125ml/4 fl oz water (omit if using powdered)

200g/7oz full fat cream cheese

200ml/6 fl oz whipping cream

25g/1oz chopped pistachios

Preparation time: 30 minutes
Setting time: 2 hours
Nutritional value:
Analysis per serving, approx:
- 3100kJ/740kcal
- 13g protein
- 44g fat
- 61g carbohydrate

Crush the rusks with a rolling pin and mix with the cinnamon. • Melt the nougat over a pan of simmering water, mix with the rusk crumbs and divide between 4 stainless steel rings or ramekins to form bases with slightly raised edges. • Scald the peaches and skin, halve and stone them. • Put the peach halves in a pan with the vanilla pod, split in half lengthwise, and mix with the sugar, lemon juice and rind, and sherry. Cover the pan and simmer for five minutes. Remove peach halves and reserve. • Soak the leaf gelatine in the cold water. • Mix the cheese and 3 tbsps peach cooking liquid until smooth. • Whip the cream until stiff. • Squeeze the excess liquid from the gelatine and dissolve in the remaining peach liquid (if using powdered, follow directions on packet). Mix the gelatine into the cheese mixture and finally the whipped cream. • Fill the nougat bases with this mixture, top with a sliced peach and put in the refrigerator to set. If using the rings, unmould and gently press the pastachios into the sides of the tarts. If serving in the ramekins, simply sprinkle the nuts over the top.

Jellies made with Exotic Fruits

Take advantage of fruits in season

Wine Jelly with Cape Gooseberries
top left

8 leaves of gelatine or 1 packet powdered
250ml/8 fl oz water (omit if using powdered)
450g/1lb Cape gooseberries
4 tbsps icing sugar
150g/5½oz sugar
125ml/4 fl oz freshly squeezed lemon juice
350ml/14 fl oz dry white wine

Preparation time: 40 minutes
Setting time: 4 hours
Nutritional value:
Analysis per serving, approx:
• 1300kJ/310kcal
• 8g protein
• 0g fat
• 63g carbohydrate

Soak the leaf gelatine in the water. • Top and tail the gooseberries, wash and dry them and prick several times, using a needle. Sift icing sugar over the berries, making sure each is well coated, cover and leave to steep. • Mix the sugar and lemon juice and heat gently in a shallow saucepan, stirring, until the sugar is dissolved. • Squeeze the liquid from the gelatine and mix into the hot lemon juice, but on no account allow the lemon juice to boil (if using powdered, follow directions on packet). • Remove the saucepan from the heat and gradually stir the wine into the lemon juice. • Leave to cool, stirring frequently. As soon as the liquid begins to set, mix in the berries. Transfer the jelly to a glass bowl which has been rinsed with cold water, cover and place in the refrigerator to set. • Shortly before serving, dip the bowl briefly in hot water and loosen the edge of the jelly with a knife. Turn out onto a serving dish and serve immediately.

Orange Jelly with Papaya
top right

8 leaves of gelatine or 1 packet powdered
250ml/8 fl oz water (omit if using powdered)
500ml/16 fl oz freshly pressed juice of blood oranges
150g/5½oz sugar
2 ripe papayas
1 tbsp lemon juice

Preparation time: 40 minutes
Setting time: 4 hours
Nutritional value:
Analysis per serving, approx:
• 1210kJ/290kcal
• 6g protein
• 0g fat
• 63g carbohydrate

Soak the leaf gelatine in the water. • Dissolve the sugar in the orange juice. • Cut the papayas in half, remove the pips, and take out the flesh using a small spoon or a melon baller. Sprinkle with the lemon juice, cover and set aside. • Heat up about one cup of orange juice. Squeeze the liquid from the leaf gelatine and dissolve in the hot juice but do not allow to boil (if using powdered, follow directions on packet). Remove the saucepan from the heat and gradually stir in the rest of the orange juice. • Leave the jelly to cool, stirring frequently. As soon as the liquid begins to set, mix in the berries. • Transfer the jelly to a glass bowl which has been rinsed with cold water, cover and place in the refrigerator to set. • Shortly before serving, dip the bowl briefly in hot water and loosen the edge of the jelly with a knife. Turn out onto a serving dish and serve immediately.

Raspberry Charlotte

A classic dessert which must be made with really fresh fruit

Ingredients for one 18cm/7-inch soufflé dish:

FOR THE CHARLOTTE:

350g/11oz crème fraîche
400g/14oz raspberries
5 leaves of gelatine or 2½ tsps powdered
250ml/8 fl oz water (omit if using powdered)
1 vanilla pod
250ml/8 fl oz milk
Pinch of salt
4 tbsps sugar
4 egg yolks
1 tsp butter
1 tsp sugar
21 sponge fingers

FOR THE SAUCE:

400g/14oz raspberries
2 tbsps icing sugar
1 tbsp lemon juice
200ml/6 fl oz raspberry liqueur

Preparation time: 1 hour
Chilling time: 12 hours
Nutritional value:
Analysis per serving (serves 8):
- 2180kJ/520kcal
- 13g protein
- 34g fat
- 39g carbohydrate

Chill the crème fraîche in the refrigerator before use. • Wash the raspberries in a bowl of water and skim the dirt from the surface, then drain them in a sieve. • Soak the leaf gelatine in the cold water. • Split the vanilla pod lengthwise and scrape out the inside with a knife. • Bring the milk, the vanilla and pod halves, salt and sugar to the boil, stirring all the time. Remove from the heat and stir in the egg yolks one at a time. Return the milk to the heat and continue stirring until the mixture thickens, but do not allow it to boil. • Squeeze the liquid from the gelatine, blend into the hot mixture and allow it to cool, stirring frequently (if using powdered, follow directions on packet). • Refrigerate the mixture until it sets. • Brush the base and sides of the dish with butter and sprinkle with the sugar. Arrange the sponge fingers vertically around the round edge facing outwards. Reserve one sponge finger. • Whisk the crème fraîche. Also whisk the egg mixture and stir into the crème fraîche, little by little, until it is well blended. • Place one-third of the mixture in the dish which has been lined with sponge fingers. Next add a layer of the raspberries followed by another layer of the cream mixture, the remaining raspberries and finishing with the remaining mixture. • Crumble the one remaining sponge finger and sprinkle over the top. • Cover the mould and leave in the refrigerator, preferably overnight, but for at least six hours. • To make the sauce: wash and drain the 400g/14oz raspberries. Keep about 20 raspberries for decoration. • Strain the other raspberries through a fine sieve and mix with the icing sugar, lemon juice and raspberry liqueur, or purée it all in a food processor or liquidiser. • Shortly before serving, dip the bowl briefly in hot water, turn out the charlotte onto a serving plate and decorate the top with the remaining raspberries. Serve the fruit sauce as an accompaniment.

Frozen Desserts

From simple basic recipes to special iced puddings
and new, original combinations – plenty of ideas
for hot summer days

Vanilla Ice Cream with an Ice-Cream Maker

The results can be as good as professional soft ice cream

Ingredients for 8 portions:

1 vanilla pod
1 egg
5 egg yolks
150g/5¹/₂oz sugar
Generous pinch of salt
4 tbsps orange flower water
500ml/16 fl oz milk
250ml/8 fl oz cream
1 tbsp crystallised violets to decorate

Preparation time: 1 hour
Freezing time: 20 minutes
Nutritional value:
Analysis per serving, approx:
- 1470kJ/350kcal
- 14g protein
- 33g fat
- 23g carbohydrate

Split the vanilla pod lengthways and scrape out the inside. • Mix the egg, egg yolks, half the sugar, the vanilla, salt and orange flower water in a metal bowl and beat, with an electric beater, over a pan of simmering water until creamy. • Bring the milk, cream and remaining sugar to the boil, stirring constantly, and gradually add the egg-and-sugar mixture while still beating. Stand the bowl of ice cream in a pan of cold water to which ice cubes have been added and stir the ice cream frequently until cold. • Place in the ice cream maker and follow the instructions for freezing until the ice is thick and creamy. This takes about 20 minutes. • Scoop the ice cream into individual sundae glasses and decorate with crystallised violets.

Our Tip: Professional ice cream manufacturers used to heat the custard to 85°C/185°F before chilling. To test the consistency, a little of the mixture was spooned up; if it formed peaks when blown on, the ice cream was ready. It is no longer necessary to do this, but it is still important to stir constantly and to freeze the mixture in an ice cream maker.

Ice Cream with Nuts or Chocolate

Classic recipes also prepared in an ice-cream maker

Nut Ice Cream
top left

Ingredients for 8 portions:
100g/4oz shelled hazelnuts	
1/2 vanilla pod	
1 egg	
4 egg yolks	
150g/5 1/2oz sugar	
500ml/16 fl oz milk	
250ml/8 fl oz cream	
100g/4oz nut paste	

Preparation time: 1 1/4 hours
Freezing time: 20 minutes
Nutritional value:
Analysis per serving, approx:
• 2300kJ/550kcal
• 15g protein
• 40g fat
• 33g carbohydrate

Roast the hazelnuts in a dry pan turning constantly until the brown skins burst. • Rub the nuts in a tea-towel until all the skins have come off. Grind or chop finely. • Split the vanilla pod lengthways and scrape out the inside. • Beat the egg, egg yolks, half the sugar and the vanilla in a metal bowl over a pan of simmering water until creamy, using an electric beater. • Bring the milk, cream and the rest of the sugar to the boil, stirring constantly, and dissolve the nut paste. • Slowly add the boiling liquid to the egg and sugar mixture over the simmering water, still beating with the electric beater. Add the chopped or ground hazelnuts. Prepare a bowl of ice water, containing ice cubes. Stand the bowl of ice cream mixture in the bowl of ice water and stir frequently until cold. • Place the mixture in the ice cream maker and follow the instructions for freezing until the ice cream is thick and creamy. This will take about 20 minutes.

Chocolate Ice Cream
top right

Ingredients for 8 portions:
225g/1oz plain chocolate	
2 eggs	
2 egg yolks	
100g/4oz sugar	
750ml/24 fl oz milk	
2 tsps instant coffee powder	
2 tbsps orange liqueur	

Preparation time: 40 minutes
Freezing time: 20 minutes
Nutritional value:
Analysis per serving, approx:
• 1590kJ/380kcal
• 12g protein
• 23g fat
• 32g carbohydrate

Break the chocolate into small pieces. • Use an electric beater and a metal bowl to beat the eggs, egg yolks and half the sugar until creamy. • Bring the milk and the rest of the sugar to the boil, stirring. Dissolve the chocolate and coffee powder in the milk. • Slowly add the boiling milk to the egg-and-sugar mixture, using a whisk. Prepare a bowl of ice water, containing ice cubes. Stand the bowl of ice cream mixture in the bowl of ice water and stir frequently until cold. • Place the cold mixture in the ice cream maker and follow the maker's instructions for freezing until thick and creamy. Towards the end of the freezing time, pour the orange liqueur into the rotating drum and mix into the ice cream for two to three minutes.

Our Tip: Decorate the ice cream with chopped hazelnuts, grated chocolate or chocolate caraque, as desired.

Red Wine Ice Cream

An unusual and delicious iced dessert

Ingredients for 8 200ml/6 fl oz ramekins:

| 2 leaves or ¹/₄ tsp powdered gelatine |
| 125ml/4 fl oz water |
| 4 egg yolks |
| 150g/5¹/₂oz raw cane sugar |
| 125ml/4 fl oz dry red wine |
| Grated rind of ¹/₂ orange |
| 1 tsp ground cinnamon |
| Pinch of ground cloves |
| 2 egg whites |
| 200ml/6 fl oz whipping cream |

Preparation time: 1 hour
Freezing time: 5 hours
Nutritional value:
Analysis per serving, approx:
• 1510kJ/360kcal
• 12g protein
• 24g fat
• 19g carbohydrate

Soak the leaf gelatine in the cold water, if using. • Beat the egg yolks in a bowl with 100g/4oz raw cane sugar, the red wine, orange rind, ¹/₂ tsp cinnamon and the cloves. Stand the bowl in a pan filled with hot water; do not allow any of the water to get into the mixture. • Whisk the mixture with an electric beater over the boiling water, until it forms a stiff foam. The mixture must never be allowed to boil. • As soon as it is firm and hot remove the pan from the hot water. Squeeze the gelatine (if using powdered gelatine, follow directions on packet) and stir into the mixture until fully dissolved. • Now allow the mixture to cool, whisking frequently. • Whisk the egg whites until they form soft peaks. Slowly add about a third of the remaining sugar and continue whisking until the egg whites are stiff and shiny. • Whip the cream until it starts to stiffen, then slowly add the second third of the sugar and continue whipping until stiff. • Fold the whipped cream and egg whites into the cooled wine mixture. • Fill the ramekins with the mixture, smooth over and freeze for five hours at -18°C/0°F. • Mix the remaining sugar with the rest of the cinnamon and sprinkle over the ice before serving.

Our Tip: This is particularly good combined with other flavours of ice cream. One scoop per portion will make a delicious topping for a refreshing fruit salad. If whipped cream is piped onto the ice cream, mix the cinnamon sugar into the cream before beating. If the ice cream is meant for a children's party, replace the red wine with freshly-squeezed orange juice or with fresh raspberry juice.

Raspberry Bombe Glacée

A decorative, traditional ending to a special meal

Ingredients for a 1.4l/2¹/₂-pint mould:

400g/14oz raspberries
5 tbsps raspberry liqueur
2 tbsps sugar
500ml/16 fl oz whipping cream
4 eggs
100g/4oz sugar
2 tbsps vanilla sugar
50g/2oz plain chocolate
1 tsp cocoa powder
125ml/4 fl oz cream, whipped
50g/2oz crystallised fruits

Preparation time: 1 hour
Freezing time: 14 hours
Nutritional value:
Analysis per serving (serves 8):
- 1970kJ/470kcal
- 9g protein
- 37g fat
- 35g carbohydrate

Wash and drain the raspberries; add half to the liqueur, cover and reserve. • Mix the other raspberries with the sugar. • Whip the 16 fl oz cream until stiff. Mix the eggs and sugar over a pan of simmering water, beating until thick. Remove from the heat and fold in the 16 fl oz whipped cream. • Mix a third of the resulting cream with the vanilla sugar, place in a metal bowl and leave to set in the freezer. • Finely grate the chocolate and stir into the second third of the mixture with the cocoa powder. • Strain the sugared raspberries through a sieve. Mix the raspberry purée into the rest of the cream mixture. Place both mixtures in separate metal bowls and leave to set in the freezer. • Spoon the semi-frozen vanilla mixture into a well-chilled bombe mould and place in the freezer for 30 minutes. • Spread the chocolate cream over the vanilla cream and freeze for 30 minutes, then add the raspberry cream. • Scrape out a hollow in the middle of the final layer and fill it with the marinated raspberries; cover with the ice cream scrapings. • Freeze the bombe glacée for about 12 hours. Turn out the bombe glacée and decorate with the cream and fruit.

Poire Hélène

This pear dish is world famous

125ml/4 fl oz water
1 tbsp sugar
1/2 cinnamon stick
1 tbsp lemon juice
2 large pears
100g/4oz cooking chocolate
200ml/6 fl oz cream
1 tbsp cognac
500g/1lb 2oz vanilla ice cream
12 crystallised violets

Preparation time: 40 minutes
Nutritional value:

Analysis per serving, approx:
• 2600kJ/620kcal
• 7g protein
• 53g fat
• 66g carbohydrate

Put the water, sugar, cinnamon and lemon juice in a saucepan, cover, and simmer gently. • Wash, dry, peel, halve and core the pears. Simmer the pears, covered, for 8 to 12 minutes, depending on size and ripeness, and then leave to cool in the cooking juice. • Cut the chocolate into small pieces and gently heat with the cream, stirring constantly, until it melts. Remove from the heat and add the cognac. • Place a pear half, cut side upwards, in each of four sundae glasses. Place a scoop of ice cream in each. Pour the warm chocolate sauce over them. • Decorate with the crystallised violets.

Our Tip: Crystallised violets are the classic decoration for this dessert. They may be left out or replaced by finely diced crystallised ginger mixed into the chocolate sauce.

Peach Melba

Normally made with raspberries, but especially good with redcurrants

400g/14oz raspberries or redcurrants
2 tbsps icing sugar
1 tbsp lemon juice
4 tbsps Cassis (blackcurrant liqueur)
4 ripe fresh peaches
500g/1lb 2oz vanilla ice cream

Preparation time: 20 minutes
Nutritional value:

Analysis per serving, approx:
• 1510kJ/360kcal
• 6g protein
• 13g fat
• 48g carbohydrate

Wash and drain the raspberries or redcurrants, strain through a sieve and mix with the icing sugar, lemon juice and Cassis. • Prick the peaches several times with a fork, dip in boiling water, peel off the skin, cut in half and remove the stone. • Place two peach halves, cut sides upwards, in dessert bowls. • Fill each peach half with a scoop of ice cream. • Pour raspberry sauce over the ice cream and peaches.

Our Tip: This dessert may also be decorated with piped cream and sprinkled with roasted flaked almonds. Peach Melba tastes particularly delicious if the sauce is prepared from fresh berries. If these are not in season you can mix 400g/14oz raspberry jam or redcurrant jelly with two tbsps raspberry liqueur. Warm the mixture briefly and strain it through a sieve.

Ice Cream with Fruit

Red Wine Pears with Vanilla Ice Cream

top left

1 lemon	
500ml/16 fl oz dry red wine	
100g/4oz sugar	
1 cinnamon stick	
4 small firm pears	
500g/1lb 2oz vanilla ice cream	

Preparation time: 20 minutes
Cooking time: 50 minutes
Nutritional value:
Analysis per serving, approx:
- 1890kJ/450kcal
- 8g protein
- 13g fat
- 60g carbohydrate

Wash and dry the lemon, slice it and put in an uncovered saucepan with the red wine, sugar and cinnamon stick. Boil until the liquid has reduced slightly. •

Wash, dry and peel the pears, using a sharp knife to cut out the cores from the underside. Leave the stalks on the pears if possible. • Remove the cinnamon stick and lemon from the red wine. Stand the pears vertically in a suitable saucepan, add the red wine and cover with a lid; gently simmer for 30 minutes. • Remove the pears, drain them, reserving the liquid, and leave to cool. Boil the red wine liquid until syrupy, in an uncovered saucepan. Allow to cool. • Cut the ice cream into cubes and place in four dessert bowls. Arrange the pears on the ice cream and pour the red wine syrup over them.

Chocolate Banana Sundae

top right

3 egg yolks	
1 tbsp vanilla sugar	
100g/4oz sugar	
150g/5½oz plain chocolate	
½ tsp cornflour	
1 tsp cocoa powder	
350ml/14 fl oz milk	
250ml/8 fl oz whipping cream	
2 ripe bananas	
1 tbsp lemon juice	
50g/2oz dried banana chips	
25g/1 oz chocolate shavings	

Preparation time: 45 minutes
Freezing time: 2 hours
Nutritional value:
Analysis per serving, approx:
- 2600kJ/620kcal
- 19g protein
- 66g fat
- 85g carbohydrate

Beat the egg yolks with the vanilla sugar and 75g/3oz sugar until fluffy. • Coarsely grate the chocolate, fold into the egg yolks with the cornflour and cocoa powder and slowly add the milk. Heat the mixture gently, whisking constantly, and bring to the boil. Remove from the heat at once. • Place the saucepan in a bowl of ice water containing ice cubes, and stir until the mixture has cooled. • Beat 125ml/4 fl oz cream with the remaining sugar until stiff and fold into the cooled chocolate mixture. Cover with foil and leave in the freezer for two hours until set. • During the first 30 minutes stir the ice cream twice. • Peel the bananas, mash with a fork and mix with the lemon juice. • Whip the remaining cream until stiff and mix with the bananas. • Place the ice cream in sundae glasses and decorate with the banana cream, banana chips and chocolate shavings.

Ice Creams with a Refreshing Flavour

Lemons and gooseberries set the tone

Lemon Yogurt Ice Cream
top left

3 eggs
100g/4oz sugar
2 lemons
300g/10oz creamy yogurt
125ml/4 fl oz cream
1 lime

Preparation time: 30 minutes
Freezing time: 2 hours
Nutritional value:
Analysis per serving, approx:
• 1590kJ/380kcal
• 14g protein
• 22g fat
• 35g carbohydrate

Separate the eggs. • Beat the egg yolks with the sugar until fluffy. • Wash and dry the lemons; grate the rind of one lemon and extract the juice from both. • Mix the yogurt with the lemon rind and juice and add to the egg yolk mixture. • Whisk the egg whites until stiff and then whip the cream likewise. • Fold both egg whites and whipped cream into the lemon mixture. Place the mixture in a metal bowl, cover with foil and freeze for two hours until solid. • Scoop out portions of ice cream and place in four dessert bowls. • Wash the lime in hot water, dry, slice thinly and quarter each slice. Use to decorate the lemon ice cream.

Gooseberry Ice Cream with Mango Foam
top right

500g/1lb 2oz gooseberries
2 tbsps lemon juice
100g/4oz icing sugar
100g/4oz crème fraîche
3 egg whites
125ml/4 fl oz water
125g/5oz sugar
1 mango
5 tbsps dry sparkling wine
1 sprig lemon balm or lemon mint

Preparation time: 45 minutes
Freezing time: 3 hours
Nutritional value:
Analysis per serving, approx:
• 2100kJ/480kcal
• 11g protein
• 12g fat
• 82g carbohydrate

Wash the gooseberries, top and tail them and put into a saucepan with the lemon juice and 125ml/4 fl oz water, cover; simmer gently for 10 minutes. Cool and strain through a sieve. • Mix the icing sugar and crème fraîche with the purée. • Whisk two egg whites until stiff and fold into the cold fruit purée. • Place the mixture in a metal bowl, cover with foil and freeze for three hours until solid. During the first half hour stir the purée twice. • Boil the water and sugar for 10 minutes to form a syrup; remove it from the heat and leave to cool. • Shortly before serving, peel the mango and slice the flesh from the stone. Purée with the wine in a liquidiser or food processor. Beat the remaining egg white and fold into the cold sugar syrup • Scoop the ice cream into individual sundae glasses and pour the mango foam over it. Wash and pat dry the lemon balm leaves and sprinkle them over the dessert.

Ice Cream Surprises

These can be prepared with or without an ice-cream maker

Tea Ice Cream with Pineapple

top left

125ml/4 fl oz milk	
3 tsps black tea leaves	
2 egg yolks	
5 tbsps sugar	
1 tbsp rum	
250ml/8 fl oz whipping cream	
1 small pineapple	
25g/1oz plain chocolate	

Preparation time: 1 hour
Freezing time: 4 hours
Nutritional value:
Analysis per serving, approx:
• 2510kJ/600kcal
• 12g protein
• 39g fat
• 47g carbohydrate

Bring the milk to the boil, pour it over the tea leaves and leave for four minutes to infuse. Strain through a tea strainer. •

Beat the egg yolks and sugar until fluffy, preferably using an electric beater, and mix in the tea-milk and rum, still beating hard. • Whip the cream until stiff, add to the tea mixture and place in a metal bowl. Cover with aluminium foil and freeze for four hours or until solid. • Cut the woody end and the crown from the pineapple and slice the fruit into eight rings of equal thickness. Peel them and cut out the central core. Cover the pineapple rings and place in the refrigerator. • Grate the chocolate coarsely. • Place two of pineapple rings on each individual plate. Use a scoop or a spoon to arrange scoops of ice cream on the pineapple rings. Decorate with the grated chocolate.

Coconut and Date Ice Cream

top right

100g/4oz flaked coconut	
100g/4oz stoned dates	
150ml/5 fl oz milk	
80g/3oz honey	
200ml/6 fl oz cream	
3 eggs	

Preparation time: 40 minutes
Freezing time: 25 minutes
Nutritional value:
Analysis per serving, approx:
• 2300kJ/550kcal
• 13g protein
• 30g fat
• 55g carbohydrate

Roast the coconut flakes in a heavy-based frying pan without fat, turning constantly until they begin to darken and give off an aroma. • Spread them out on a plate and leave to cool. •

Cut the dates into pieces. • Mix the coconut, dates, milk, honey, cream and eggs for one minute in a liquidiser or food processor. Put the mixture into the drum of the ice cream maker and follow the maker's instructions to freeze to a thick creamy consistency; this will take about 25 minutes.

Our Tip: If you do not have a liquidiser or food processor, you will have to use a sharp knife to cut up the dates as finely as possible. Then use an electric beater to mix thoroughly with the other ingredients. If the ice cream is to be frozen in the freezer, place the mixture in a metal bowl, cover with aluminium foil and leave for about four hours to solidify. Remove the ice cream from the freezer and stir thoroughly, at least once an hour.

Chocolate and Nut Ice Cream with Caramel Bananas

Left-over portions can be stored for eight days in the freezer

50g/2oz shelled hazelnuts

50g/2oz plain chocolate

2 tbsps cocoa powder

½ tsp vanilla essence

50g/2oz honey

50g/2oz raw cane sugar

200ml/6 fl oz cream

250ml/8 fl oz milk

3 eggs

500g/1lb 2oz bananas

2 tbsps butter

50g/2oz raw cane sugar

Generous pinch of ground cinnamon

Preparation time: 1 hour
Freezing time: 1 hour
Nutritional value:
Analysis per serving, approx:
• 2010kJ/480kcal
• 12g protein
• 33g fat
• 56g carbohydrate

Roast the hazelnuts in a dry pan until the brown skins burst. Rub off the skins with a tea towel. Grind the nuts finely in a liquidiser or food processor. • Break the chocolate into small pieces and melt over a very low heat with the cocoa powder, vanilla, honey, sugar and cream, stirring all the time. • Blend the ground nuts with the milk, eggs and cool chocolate mixture. • Place the mixture in the drum of the ice cream maker and, following the maker's directions, freeze the ice cream for about 30 minutes. • Place the ice cream in the freezer for a further 30 minutes. • Peel the bananas and cut into thin, oblique slices. • Melt the butter until foaming in a saucepan; stir in the sugar and cinnamon and allow to caramelise slightly. • Cook the banana slices in the caramelised butter mixture for five minutes, stirring frequently. • Scoop out eight portions (about half) the ice cream and arrange on four individual dishes or plates, top with the hot banana slices and sprinkle with the caramel.

Exquisite Fruit Parfaits

Fresh ripe fruit tastes best in these desserts

Mango-Plum Parfait
top left

Ingredients for 8 portions:

1 ripe mango, about 300g/10oz
3 eggs
70g/3oz raw cane sugar
20g/³⁄₄oz finely chopped crystallised ginger
Grated rind of 1 orange
5 tbsps egg nog
350ml/14 fl oz whipping cream
50g/2oz shelled walnuts
200g/7oz plum jam or preserve
2 tbsps plum or other fruit brandy

Preparation time: 1¼ hours
Freezing time: 6 hours
Nutritional value:
Analysis per serving, approx:
- 1170kJ/280kcal
- 7g protein
- 24g fat
- 25g carbohydrate

Peel the mango, cut the flesh from the stone and dice. • Separate the eggs and reserve two whites for later use. • Beat the egg yolks with 40g/1½ oz sugar until fluffy. • Mix in the mango, ginger, orange peel and two tbsps of egg nog. • Whisk one egg white with 10g/¼ oz raw cane sugar until stiff. Whip 150ml/5 fl oz cream with 10g/¼ oz sugar until stiff. • Fold the egg white and whipped cream into the egg yolk mixture, place in a round metal bowl, smooth the top and freeze for two hours until thick and creamy. • Now make the plum ice cream. Roast the nuts gently in a dry frying pan and grind finely. • Whisk the remaining egg whites with the rest of the sugar until stiff. Beat the remaining cream until stiff and fold into the plum preserve; add the brandy and fold in the egg whites and the grated nuts. • Spread the plum mixture over the layer of mango, cover with aluminium foil and freeze for

a further four hours. • Turn out the parfait onto a chilled dish and sprinkle with the rest of the egg nog.

Chocolate Whisky Parfait
top right

200g/7oz milk chocolate
15g/½ oz butter
1 tsp instant coffee
3 tbsps whisky
3 egg yolks
250ml/8 fl oz whipping cream
500g/1lb 2oz ripe apricots
1 tbsp lemon juice
8 strawberries to decorate

Preparation time: 1 hour
Freezing time: 4 hours
Nutritional value:
Analysis per serving, approx:
- 2640kJ/630kcal
- 18g protein
- 61g fat
- 46g carbohydrate

Melt the chocolate and butter in a bowl over a pan of simmering water. Add the coffee, whisky and egg yolks. Remove from the pan of hot water and allow to cool. • Whip the cream until stiff and fold into the mixture. Divide between the four ramekins, cover with aluminium foil and freeze for four hours. • Place the apricots in boiling water for five minutes, skin and halve them and remove the stones. Purée in a liquidiser or food processor or strain through a fine sieve and mix with the lemon juice. • Wash, pat dry and halve or quarter the strawberries. • Divide the apricot sauce between four dessert plates and turn the parfaits out onto the sauce, decorating with the strawberries.

Ice Creams with Fruit Sauces

Delightful combinations of ice cream and fruit

Lemon Ice Cream with Rose-Hip Sauce

top left

3 lemons
3 egg yolks
2 tbsps white rum
100g/4oz sugar
250ml/8 fl oz whipping cream
200g/7oz rose-hip purée (health food shop)
2 tbsps clear honey
5 tbsps red wine

Preparation time: 40 minutes
Freezing time: 3 hours
Nutritional value:
Analysis per serving, approx:
• 2220kJ/530kcal
• 15g protein
• 44g fat
• 69g carbohydrate

Wash the lemons in warm water, dry them and grate the rind of one. Peel the other lemons very finely and cut the peel into fine julienne strips. Wrap the julienne strips in foil and place in the refrigerator. • Extract the juice from all three lemons. • Beat the egg yolks with the rum and sugar over a pan of simmering water until fluffy. • Whip the cream until stiff. • Mix the grated lemon rind and lemon juice into the egg yolk mixture and fold in the whipped cream. • Place the mixture in a metal bowl, cover with aluminium foil and freeze for three hours until set. Remove the ice cream from the freezer and stir once every hour. • Heat up the rose-hip purée with the honey and red wine, stirring all the time. • Using an ice cream scoop, place portions in individual dessert glasses and pour the rose-hip sauce over the ice cream. Decorate with the reserved strips of lemon rind.

Almond Ice Cream with Apricot Sauce

top right

Ingredients for 8 portions:
100g/4oz sultanas
4 tbsps Amaretto (Italian almond liqueur)
2 egg yolks
50g/2oz vanilla sugar
400ml/15 fl oz whipping cream
100g/4oz blanched, finely ground almonds
100g/4oz chopped almonds
100g/4oz plain chocolate
500g/1lb 2oz ripe apricots
4 tbsps apricot liqueur
1 tbsp sugar

Preparation time: 1 hour
Freezing time: 3 hours
Nutritional value:
Analysis per serving, approx:
• 2470kJ/590kcal
• 15g protein
• 55g fat
• 49g carbohydrate

Wash the sultanas in hot water, pat dry, and leave to soak in the Amaretto. • Beat the egg yolks and vanilla sugar over a pan of simmering water until fluffy. Whip the cream until stiff. • Mix the sultanas, liqueur, ground and chopped almonds into the egg yolk mixture, grate in the chocolate and fold in the whipped cream. • Transfer the mixture to a metal bowl, cover with aluminium foil and freeze for three hours until set. • Pour boiling water over the apricots, skin them and remove the stones. Reserve one for decoration and purée the others in a liquidiser or food processor with the liqueur, sugar and three tbsps water. • Slice the almond ice cream into small, even cubes and arrange in dessert bowls. Pour the apricot sauce over them and decorate with apricot slices.

Fruit Ice Creams, Imaginatively Served

Ice cream with a high cream content does not need to be stirred during the freezing process

Raspberry Ice Cream with Pistachio Cream
top left

500g/1lb 2oz raspberries	
100g/4oz sugar	
600ml/18 fl oz whipping cream	
1 tsp lemon juice	
1 tbsp vanilla sugar	
25g/1oz chopped pistachios	

Preparation time: 30 minutes
Marinating time: 2 hours
Freezing time: 3 hours
Nutritional value:
Analysis per serving, approx:
• 2730kJ/650kcal
• 6g protein
• 52g fat
• 45g carbohydrate

Wash the raspberries several times in a bowl of water and skim off any dirt from the surface. Drain the raspberries. • Mix with the sugar in a bowl, mash with a fork and cover. Refrigerate for two hours. • Beat two-thirds of the cream until stiff. • Strain the raspberries through a fine sieve and mix with the lemon juice. Fold the purée into the whipped cream, empty into a metal bowl and cover with aluminium foil; leave to set for three hours in the freezer. • Shortly before serving, whip the rest of the cream and vanilla sugar until stiff and put into a piping bag with a star nozzle. • Arrange scoops of ice cream in four dessert bowls. Decorate with rosettes of cream and the pistachios.

Orange Ice Cream with Orange Sauce
top right

3 egg yolks	
100g/4oz sugar	
200ml/6 fl oz whipping cream	
1 orange	
2 tbsps Grand Marnier	
1 orange	
1 tsp cornflour	
50g/2oz sugar	
3 tbsps Grand Marnier	
4 tbsps chocolate shavings	

Preparation time: 50 minutes
Freezing time: 3 hours
Nutritional value:
Analysis per serving, approx:
• 2310kJ/550kcal
• 15g protein
• 43g fat
• 55g carbohydrate

Beat the egg yolks and sugar in a bowl over a pan of hot water until the mixture is hot and creamy. • Remove the bowl to a pan of cold water and continue whisking the mixture until completely cool. • Whip the cream until stiff. • Squeeze the juice from the orange and stir into the egg yolk mixture with the 2 tbsps liqueur and whipped cream. • Place the mixture in a metal loaf tin, cover with foil and freeze for three hours or until set. • To make the sauce, squeeze the remaining orange; take two tbsps of the juice and blend with the cornflour. • Stirring constantly, heat up the rest of the orange juice with the sugar until it boils; add the cornflour liquid and extra liqueur. Bring to the boil again, remove from the heat and allow to cool. • Briefly dip the loaf tin in cold water, unmould the ice cream and pour the orange sauce over it. Before serving, sprinkle with chocolate shavings.

Cassis Ice Cream

A festive conclusion to a special meal

Ingredients for six 200ml/6 fl oz ramekins:
500g/1lb 2oz blackcurrants
150g/5¹/₂oz raw cane sugar
100ml/3 fl oz unsweetened blackcurrant juice (health food shop)
1 tbsp lemon juice
400ml/15 fl oz whipping cream
6 tbsps cassis (blackcurrant liqueur)

Preparation time: 30 minutes
Freezing time: 3 hours
Nutritional value:
Analysis per serving, approx:
- 1600kJ/380kcal
- 3g protein
- 21g fat
- 39g carbohydrate

Wash the blackcurrants and drain on absorbent kitchen paper. Set aside six small sprigs and reserve in the refrigerator. • Remove the stalks from the other berries. • Bring the raw cane sugar and the blackcurrant juice to the boil, stirring constantly. Add the blackcurrants and simmer, covered, on a low heat for five minutes. • Mash the berries with a fork, strain through a fine sieve and mix with the lemon juice. Cool, cover and chill in the refrigerator. • Whip 300ml/9 fl oz cream until stiff and fold into the fruit purée. Pour into the ramekins, cover with aluminium foil and leave in the freezer for three hours to set. • Whip the remaining cream until stiff and place in a piping bag with a star nozzle. • Dip the ramekins in cold water. Turn out the ice cream onto plates, decorate with the blackcurrant sprigs and rosettes of cream. Sprinkle each portion with cassis.

Melon Ice Cream with Almond Sauce

Especially good when made in an ice-cream maker

FOR THE ICE CREAM:
1 ripe honeydew melon (600g/1lb 6oz)
125ml/4 fl oz each of milk and double cream
100g/4oz honey
Juice and grated rind of ¹/₂ lemon
¹/₂ tsp vanilla essence

FOR THE ALMOND SAUCE:
50g/2oz blanched almonds
2 tbsps honey
7 tbsps cream

Preparation time: 1 hour
Freezing time: 1 hour
Nutritional value:
Analysis per serving, approx:
- 1800kJ/430kcal
- 6g protein
- 24g fat
- 50g carbohydrate

Cut the melon in half lengthways, remove the seeds and pith and scoop one half of the flesh from the rind. • Cut the flesh into fairly large chunks and purée in a liquidiser or food processor with the milk, cream, honey, lemon rind and juice and the vanilla, or strain through a fine sieve. • Put the fruit mixture in the drum of the ice cream maker and follow the maker's instructions to freeze it for 15 to 30 minutes. • Place the ice cream in the freezer for a further 30 minutes. • Separate the remaining fruit flesh from the rind with a melon baller. • Shortly before serving, chop the almonds and roast in a dry frying-pan, turning frequently until they begin to darken. • Mix the honey into the almonds and allow to caramelise slightly, then gradually add the cream. • Scoop or spoon out the melon ice cream onto four dessert plates, add the melon balls and coat with the almond sauce.

Chocolate Ice Cream Roll

Freezes well – a useful standby for unexpected guests

Ingredients for 1 roll:

For the ice cream:

6 egg yolks

75g/3oz sugar

150g/5¹/₂oz plain chocolate

250ml/8 fl oz whipping cream

For the roll:

8 egg yolks

100g/4oz sugar

4 egg whites

80g/3oz flour

20g/³/₄oz cornflour

100ml/3 fl oz whipping cream

1 tbsp vanilla sugar

2 tbsps chocolate strands

Preparation time: 45 minutes
Freezing time: 3 hours
Baking: 12 minutes
Nutritional value:
Analysis per serving (serves 12):
- 2390kJ/570kcal
- 20g protein
- 41g fat
- 28g carbohydrate

Beat the egg yolks and sugar until fluffy. • Break the chocolate into pieces and melt with half the cream. Cool and beat into the egg yolk mixture until it thickens. • Whip the rest of the cream until stiff and fold into the chocolate mixture. • Cover with aluminium foil and freeze for two hours. • Meanwhile, make the sponge. Heat the oven to 220°C/425°F/Gas Mark 7. Line the baking sheet with baking parchment. • Beat the egg yolks and sugar until fluffy. Whisk the egg whites until stiff and fold into the egg yolk mixture with the flour and cornflour. • Spread the mixture onto the baking sheet and bake for 12 minutes until golden. • Turn out the sponge onto a tea towel sprinkled with sugar, pull off the paper and cover the sponge with a damp cloth; leave to cool. • Allow the ice cream to soften slightly and spread it over the sponge. • Roll up the sponge and return it to the freezer. • Whip the cream and vanilla sugar until stiff, spread it on the sponge roll and decorate with chocolate strands.

Omelette Surprise

A surprise dessert from France

Ingredients for 10 portions:

7 eggs
100g/4oz caster sugar
Grated rind of 1 lemon
1 tbsp cognac
100g/4oz flour
25g/1oz each of chopped almonds and chopped pistachios
20 scoops of ice cream and sorbet (mixed flavours)
100g/4oz icing sugar, sifted

Preparation time: 40 minutes
Baking time: 12 to 15 minutes
Freezing time: 30 minutes
Nutritional value:
Analysis per serving, approx:
- 1840kJ/440kcal
- 14g protein
- 21g fat
- 46g carbohydrate

Heat the oven to 200°C/400°F/Gas Mark 6. Line a rectangular tin with baking parchment. • Separate the eggs and reserve three of the whites. • Beat the egg yolks with the sugar and lemon rind until fluffy and add the cognac. • Sift the flour into the egg yolk mixture and mix gently. Whisk the four egg whites until stiff and fold into the egg yolks. Spread the mixture evenly over the lined baking tin. • Scatter the almonds and pistachios over the sponge and bake for 12 to 15 minutes until golden; then leave to cool. • Line the bottom of an oblong ovenproof dish with sponge cut to fit. • Arrange the scoops of ice cream over it and cover with the rest of the sponge. • Place the mould in the freezer for 30 minutes so that ice cream does not melt. • Heat the oven to 225°C/425°F/Gas Mark 7. • Whisk the remaining egg whites until stiff, sift 50g/2oz icing sugar over them and fold in. Fold in the other half of the sifted icing sugar and put this meringue into a piping bag with a star nozzle. • Completely cover the sponge in the mould with egg whites. Place the egg whites on the uppermost shelf of the oven and bake for 4 to 7 minutes until golden. • Serve the omelette at once.

Sophisticated Ice Cream Desserts

With a little care the results can look very professional

Neapolitan Ice Cream Gateau
top left

Ingredients for 1 26cm/10-inch rectangular loaf tin:

250g/8oz strawberries, washed	
3 tbsps vanilla sugar	
10 eggs	
150g/5½oz sugar	
750ml/24 fl oz whipping cream	
100g/4oz plain chocolate	
2 tbsps rum	

Preparation time: 1 hour
Freezing time: 5 hours
Nutritional value:
Analysis per serving (serves 8):
• 960kJ/230kcal
• 7g protein
• 16g fat
• 14g carbohydrate

Purée the strawberries with one tbsp vanilla sugar. • Separate the eggs. Beat the yolks and sugar until creamy. Whisk the whites until stiff. • Whip the cream until stiff and fold into the egg yolk mixture, then fold in the egg whites. Divide this mixture into thirds and put in separate bowls. Mix the rest of the vanilla sugar into one third, place in the mould and leave to set in the freezer. • Mix the strawberries with the second third, pour over the vanilla mixture and return to the freezer. • Melt the chocolate over a pan of hot water, leave to cool slightly, then mix with the rum into the final third of the mixture. Pour this over the strawberry mixture and return to the freezer for at least five hours.

Cassata
top right

Ingredients for 10 portions:

6 eggs • 180g/6oz icing sugar	
1 tbsp vanilla sugar	
100g/4oz flour	
75g/3oz cornflour	
200g/7oz mixed crystallised fruit	
100g/4oz plain chocolate	
500g/1lb 2oz ricotta	
150g/5½oz sugar	
4 tbsps Maraschino liqueur	
8 tbsps Marsala wine	
125ml/4 fl oz whipping cream	

Preparation time: 1 hour
Baking time: 25 minutes
Freezing time: 1 to 2 hours
Nutritional value:
Analysis per serving, approx:
• 1910kJ/440kcal
• 12g protein
• 32g fat
• 49g carbohydrate

Heat the oven to 200°C/400°F/Gas Mark 6. • Separate the eggs. Beat the yolks with the icing sugar and vanilla sugar until fluffy. Whisk the egg whites until stiff and fold into the egg yolk mixture. • Sift the flour and cornflour onto the mixture and fold. • Spread the mixture over a baking sheet lined with baking parchment and bake for 12 minutes until golden. • Turn out the sponge onto a tea towel sprinkled with sugar, pull off the paper and cover the sponge with a damp cloth; leave to cool. • Set aside some of the crystallised fruit for decoration and dice the rest with the chocolate. • Mix the ricotta with the sugar, liqueur and fruit and chocolate mixture. • Cut the sponge into strips, sprinkle with Marsala and use to line a rectangular loaf tin. • Spread the ricotta mixture over the sponge, cover it with the rest of the sponge strips and sprinkle with some more Marsala. • Place the cassata in the freezer and freeze for at least five hours. • Remove from the freezer about 15 minutes before serving. Whip the cream until stiff. Dip the loaf tin briefly in hot water and unmould onto a board. Cut in slices and decorate with the whipped cream and crystallised fruit.

Ice Cream Surprises

More great ideas for refreshing iced treats

Blackberry Ice Cream with a White Chocolate Sauce
top left

Ingredients for 6 portions:

300g/10oz blackberries
3 eggs
100g/4oz sugar
1 tbsp vanilla sugar
Pinch of cardamom
350ml/14 fl oz whipping cream
200g/7oz white chocolate
2 tbsps white rum

Preparation time: 30 minutes
Freezing time: 3 hours
Nutritional value:
Analysis per serving, approx:
• 1930kJ/460kcal
• 9g protein
• 27g fat
• 42g carbohydrate

Wash, drain, purée and sieve the blackberries. • Separate the eggs. Beat the egg yolks with the sugar, vanilla sugar and cardamom until fluffy. Place in a metal bowl, cover and leave in the freezer until almost set. • Whisk the egg whites until stiff and beat 250ml/8 fl oz cream until stiff. • Mix the blackberry purée into the egg yolk mixture and fold in the egg whites and the whipped cream; freeze for about three hours. Break the chocolate into pieces, melt over a pan of hot water and mix with the rest of the cream and the rum. • Arrange scoops of the blackberry ice cream on individual serving plates or dessert bowls. Then coat with the warm, white chocolate sauce and serve immediately.

Strawberry Cream
top right

500g/1lb 2oz strawberries
100g/4oz sugar
2 tbsps vanilla sugar
1 tbsp lemon juice
150g/5½oz yogurt
150g/5½oz crème fraîche
200ml/6 fl oz whipping cream

Preparation time: 30 minutes
Freezing time: 2½ hours
Nutritional value:
Analysis per serving, approx:
• 2100kJ/500kcal
• 5g protein
• 34g fat
• 44g carbohydrate

Wash and drain the strawberries and reserve some attractive ones for decoration. Remove the hulls from the rest and purée with the sugar, vanilla sugar and lemon juice. •

Mix the yogurt and crème fraîche and fold into the purée. Place the mixture in a metal bowl and leave, covered, for 30 minutes in the freezer, stirring twice during this period. • Whip the cream until stiff, fold it into the strawberry mixture and place in the freezer for a further two hours to set. Every half hour, remove from the freezer and beat so that the mixture remains smooth. • Arrange the strawberry ice cream in individual serving bowls and decorate with the remaining strawberries and some more whipped cream, if desired.

Iced Cheesecake

A clever invention which does not need to be baked

Ingredients for a 26cm/10-inch springform cake tin:

200g/7oz sponge fingers
50g/2oz butter
1 tbsp vanilla sugar
Generous pinch of ground cinnamon
3 egg yolks
100g/4oz icing sugar
2 tbsps lemon juice
Grated rind of ½ a lemon
500g/1lb 2oz mascarpone (Italian cream cheese)
250ml/8 fl oz whipping cream
2 tbsps cocoa powder
12 cocktail cherries

Preparation time: 45 minutes
Freezing time: 3 hours
Nutritional value:
Analysis per serving (serves 12):
- 1890kJ/450kcal
- 12g protein
- 33g fat
- 24g carbohydrate

Crush the sponge fingers with a rolling pin between sheets of cling film • Melt the butter and mix into the sponge crumbs with the vanilla sugar and cinnamon. Line the base of the tin, pressing the dough down firmly. • Beat the egg yolks with the icing sugar until fluffy and mix in the lemon juice, rind and the mascarpone. Stir 125ml/4 fl oz cream into the mixture. • Spread the mixture over the sponge base, cover with aluminium foil and freeze for about three hours to set. • Whip the remaining cream until stiff and place in a piping bag with a star nozzle. • Loosen the edge of the cheesecake from the tin with a sharp knife. Sift cocoa powder over the top and slide it onto a cake plate. Decorate with rosettes of cream and cocktail cherries.

Our Tip: Mascarpone can be replaced by any cream cheese, such as Philadelphia, but this will give a firmer consistency. To achieve the same consistency, add 200ml/6 fl oz double cream instead of 125ml/4 fl oz.

Peach Sundaes

Traditional desserts for gourmets

Peaches Escoffier
top left

2 well ripened peaches	
Juice and grated rind of 1 orange	
50g/2oz preserving sugar	
350ml/14 fl oz cream	
1/4 vanilla pod	
2 tbsps icing sugar	
4 tbsps orange liqueur (Grand Marnier)	
8 small scoops of nut ice cream (see tip)	

Preparation time: 30 minutes
Cooking time: 10 minutes
Nutritional value:
Analysis per serving, approx:
• 2310kJ/550kcal
• 6g protein
• 31g fat
• 52g carbohydrate

Dip the peaches in boiling water, skin, halve and remove the stones. • Put the peach halves in a saucepan with orange juice, two tbsps water, the orange rind and the preserving sugar. Simmer gently for 10 minutes. Drain the peaches and leave to cool. Reserve the peach syrup. • Place the cream in the freezer for 10 minutes. • Split the vanilla pod lengthways, scrape out the inside and mix with the icing sugar. • Arrange the peaches, cut side downwards, on four plates. • Mix half the cream with the orange liqueur and peach syrup and pour around the peaches. • Whip the rest of the cream with the vanilla and icing sugar mixture until stiff and use it to decorate the peaches. • Arrange scoops of the nut ice cream on the orange sauce.

Our Tip: Nut ice cream can be prepared by using a similar method to chocolate ice cream, but replace the chocolate with nut paste, and omit the coffee powder and liqueur.

Oriental Peach Promise
top right

4 ripe peaches	
3 pieces ginger in syrup	
250ml/8 fl oz white wine	
3 tbsps ginger syrup	
3 cardamom pods	
Pinch of ground nutmeg	
1/4 cinnamon stick	
2 egg yolks	
1 egg	
50g/2oz sugar	
8 small scoops of passion fruit or vanilla ice cream	

Preparation time: 30 minutes
Nutritional value:
Analysis per serving, approx:
• 2010kJ/480kcal
• 16g protein
• 32g fat
• 56g carbohydrate

Dip the peaches in boiling water, skin and halve them and remove the stones. • Dice one ginger fruit and cut the rest into fine strips. • Mix together the white wine, ginger syrup, diced ginger, crushed cardamom, nutmeg, cinnamon stick and peach halves. Cover and gently heat in a saucepan for three to four minutes. • Drain the peaches and refrigerate. • Beat the egg yolks, the egg and sugar with an electric beater until fluffy, over a pan of hot water. Strain the reserved peach syrup and add it. Continue beating until the mixture becomes hot and thick. • Place the peach halves, cut side uppermost, on four plates and fill each hollow with a scoop of ice cream. • Pour the wine cream sauce around the peaches and scatter strips of ginger over them.

Flambéed Ice Cream Parcels and a Frosted Soufflé

Magical effects for a special occasion

Flambéed Ice Cream Pancakes

top left

3 eggs	
50g/2oz flour	
125ml/4 fl oz milk	
1 tsp sugar • Pinch of salt	
15g/¹/₂ oz clarified butter	
4 small scoops each of nut, mango and lemon ice cream	
2 oranges	
8 sugar cubes	
50g/2oz butter	
2 tbsps sugar	
8 tbsps orange liqueur	

Preparation time: 1 hour
Freezing time: 30 minutes
Nutritional value:
Analysis per serving, approx:
• 2800kJ/670kcal
• 17g protein
• 38g fat
• 55g carbohydrate

Separate one of the eggs. Whisk the egg yolk with the two whole eggs, the flour, milk, sugar and salt. • Use the clarified butter to make four very thin pancakes with the batter; allow to cool. • Whisk the remaining egg white. • Place one scoop of each ice cream in the centre of each pancake. Brush the edges of the pancakes with the egg white, fold them over the ice cream and place the parcels in the freezer for 30 minutes. • Rub sugar cubes over the rind of one orange and cut half of the rind of the other orange into julienne strips; squeeze the juice from both oranges. • Melt the butter in a heavy-based pan and stir in the sugar cubes and sugar until they dissolve. Pour the orange juice into the pan and boil until it thickens. • Heat up the pancake parcels in the syrup for one minute on each side. • Pour the liqueur around the edges of the pan, set it alight and serve.

Foaming Chocolate Ice Cream

top right

Ingredients for 8 portions:

¹/₂ vanilla pod	
250ml/8 fl oz milk	
5 egg yolks	
150g/5¹/₂oz clear honey	
150g/5¹/₂oz cooking chocolate	
2 tbsps rum	
250ml/15 fl oz whipping cream	
3 tbsps Cointreau (orange liqueur)	
Grated rind of ¹/₂ orange	
4 tbsps icing sugar	

Preparation time: 1¹/₄ hours
Freezing time: 4 hours
Nutritional value:
Analysis per serving, approx:
• 1930kJ/460kcal
• 13g protein
• 43g fat
• 39g carbohydrate

Split the vanilla pod lengthways, scrape out the inside, place both in the milk and bring to the boil. Beat the egg yolks with the honey in a bowl over a pan of hot water until fluffy, then slowly add the hot milk. Continue beating until the mixture becomes creamy. • Transfer the bowl to a pan of iced water and continue whisking until cool, then refrigerate. • Melt 100g/4oz chocolate with the rum. Whip the cream until stiff. • Mix one half of the vanilla mixture with the Cointreau and orange rind and mix the other half with the slightly cooled liquid chocolate. Fold half the whipped cream into each of the mixtures. • Pour both mixtures simultaneously into a metal bowl so that they combine. • Allow the whole mass to set in the freezer for about four hours. • Sift icing sugar over eight dessert bowls. Spoon balls of ice cream over the icing sugar. Grate the remaining chocolate onto them.

Pineapple "Sarah Bernhardt"

This recipe was dedicated to one of the greatest actresses of her time

1 pineapple weighing about 800g
4 tbsps kirsch
50g/2oz preserving sugar
Juice of 1 lemon
125ml/4 fl oz white wine
1 egg
250ml/8 fl oz whipping cream
2 tsps icing sugar
2 tsps ground cinnamon
Generous pinch each of ground cardamom and ginger
8 scoops of orange ice cream
4 tbsps freshly grated chocolate

Preparation time: 40 minutes
Marinating time: 2 hours
Nutritional value:
Analysis per serving, approx:
• 2770kJ/660kcal
• 10g protein
• 39g fat
• 72g carbohydrate

Peel the pineapple and cut into eight equal, 1cm/½-inch slices. Remove the core from the middle of each slice, place the slices in a bowl, sprinkle with the kirsch, cover and marinate in the refrigerator for two hours. • Remove the hard core from the rest of the pineapple, cut the flesh into small pieces, place in a saucepan with the preserving sugar, lemon juice and white wine. Cover and simmer for five minutes over a low heat. Purée in a liquidiser or food processor with the fruit liquid and egg. • Briefly reheat the purée but do not allow it to boil. • Whip the cream with the icing sugar, cinnamon, cardamom and ginger until stiff. • Arrange the pineapple rings with the marinade on four plates and place a scoop of orange ice cream on each portion. • Mix the pineapple sauce with four tbsps cream and pour it around the pineapple. • Put the rest of the cream into a piping bag with a star nozzle and pipe it round the ice cream. Sprinkle the grated chocolate over the cream.

Mixed Fruit Ice Cream

A slimming fruit ice cream without cream which is quick to prepare

200ml/6 fl oz ice-cold dry sparkling wine or a fruit juice

75g/3oz icing sugar

400g/14oz mixed frozen berries (blackberries, strawberries, raspberries, redcurrants or blackcurrants)

2 to 4 tbsps Maraschino liqueur

A little egg nog, if desired

Preparation time: 20 minutes
Freezing time: 1 hour
Nutritional value:
Analysis per serving, approx:
• 800kJ/190kcal
• 1g protein
• 1g fat
• 29g carbohydrate

Before you begin, place a metal bowl in the freezer. • Reserve two tbsps of the frozen berries in the freezer compartment • Pour the wine or juice and the icing sugar into a liquidiser or food processor, mix briefly and gradually add the other berries while the motor is running. Purée for one minute more. Lastly, pour in the Maraschino and process briefly. • Pour the fruit purée into the ice-cold metal bowl, cover with aluminium foil and allow to set for about one hour. • Remove the berries from the freezer compartment. • Dice the fruit ice cream or use an ice cream scoop and arrange in sundae glasses. Sprinkle with the reserved frozen berries and, if desired, a little egg liqueur.

Mango Sorbet

The recipe is based on one from the Middle East

Ingredients for 8 portions:

2 to 3 mangoes

150g/5½oz caster sugar

Juice of 1 lemon

1 egg white

8 leaves of lemon balm or fresh mint

Preparation time: 30 minutes
Freezing time: about 40 minutes
Nutritional value:
Analysis per serving, approx:
• 630kJ/150kcal
• 2g protein
• 0g fat
• 36g carbohydrate

Wash and dry the mangoes. Peel them and cut the flesh from the stone. There should be 500g/1lb 2oz left. • Purée the mango with half the sugar and the lemon juice in the liquidiser or food processor, empty into the sorbetière and follow the manufacturer's instructions so that the sorbet sets in about 30 minutes. • Whisk the egg white over a pan of hot water until fluffy and pour in the rest of the sugar. Continue whisking for a further four minutes until stiff and then beat over a pan of cold water until cold. • When the sorbet is thick and creamy, mix in the egg whites and leave for five to ten minutes more to set. • Form eight portions of sorbet with an ice cream scoop, place these in wine glasses and decorate each portion with lemon balm.

Our Tip: Sorbets can be made from many kinds of fruit, vegetables and even herbs. Suitable fruits are apples, apricots, cherries, kiwi fruits, pears, pineapples, plums and all types of berry. Fruit which cannot be puréed well when raw should be peeled and stoned, then stewed until soft in a little water, sugar and the lemon juice, before puréeing.

Exotic Fruit Sorbets

Iced desserts for the "bon viveur" – if you like, pour some well-chilled dry sparkling wine over the sorbet before serving

Passion Fruit and Persimmon Sorbet

top left

250ml/8 fl oz water	
Juice of 1 lemon	
125g/5oz caster sugar	
2 fully ripe persimmons (kaki or sharon fruit)	
2 passion fruits	
2 tbsps apricot liqueur	
1 egg white	
1 tbsp vanilla sugar	

Preparation time: 45 minutes
Freezing time: 2 hours
Nutritional value:
Analysis per serving, approx:
• 1000kJ/240kcal
• 5g protein
• 0g fat
• 52g carbohydrate

Boil the water, lemon juice and sugar for five minutes, then allow to cool. • Peel the persimmons and strain through a sieve. Halve the passion fruit, scoop out the contents with a teaspoon and mix with the persimmon purée. • Mix the purée with the sugar syrup and liqueur, place in a metal bowl, cover and freeze for about an hour until nearly set, stirring at short intervals. • Whisk the egg white until fluffy, gradually pour in the vanilla sugar and continue whisking until stiff and shiny. • Fold the egg whites into the fruit purée and freeze the sorbet for another hour. • Arrange scoops of sorbet in individual dessert dishes or wine glasses.

Redcurrant and Kiwi Sorbet

top right

Ingredients for 8 portions:

250g/8oz caster sugar
100ml/3 fl oz water
300g/10oz redcurrants
4 kiwis
2 tbsps cassis (blackcurrant liqueur)
125ml/4 fl oz dry red wine
125ml/4 fl oz dry sparkling white wine
1 tbsp white rum
2 egg whites

Preparation time: 40 minutes
Freezing time: 2 hours
Nutritional value:
Analysis per serving, approx:
• 880kJ/210kcal
• 4g protein
• 0g fat
• 41g carbohydrate

Heat the sugar and water, boil for five minutes and then allow to cool. • Wash and drain the redcurrants and reserve some sprigs for decoration. Remove stalks from the rest of the redcurrants and purée also. • Peel three kiwis, cut into pieces and purée. Mix half the sugar syrup into each purée. • Add the cassis and red wine to the redcurrant purée and mix the white wine and rum into the kiwi purée. • Place both purées in separate metal bowls, cover and freeze for one hour until almost set, stirring at 15-minute intervals. • Whisk the egg whites until stiff and fold half into each of the purées. Freeze the sorbets for another hour. • Peel the fourth kiwi fruit and cut into slices. • Arrange one scoop of each sorbet in individual dessert bowls or wine glasses and decorate with slices of kiwi and the reserved redcurrants.

Cassis Sorbet in Marzipan Flowers

An unusual and attractive way to serve sorbet

Ingredients for 6 portions:

750g/1lb 10oz blackcurrants	
4 mint or lemon balm leaves	
250g/8oz icing sugar	
Juice of 1 lemon or lime	
8 tbsps maraschino liqueur	
200g/7oz marzipan	
1 egg white	
3 tbsps preserving sugar	
12 tbsps egg nog	
6 tbsps Grenadine syrup	

Preparation time: 1 hour
Freezing time: 2¹/₂ hours
Nutritional value:
Analysis per serving, approx:
• 2010kJ/480kcal
• 7g protein
• 7g fat
• 24g carbohydrate

Wash the blackcurrants and drain on absorbent paper. • Wash, pat dry and chop the mint or lemon balm. • Sift the icing sugar. • Remove stalks from the blackcurrants then pureé in a liquidiser or food processor. Strain through a fine sieve and mix with the lemon or lime juice, 200g/7oz icing sugar, the chopped herbs and six tbsps maraschino liqueur.
• Transfer the purée to a metal bowl, cover and leave to set in the freezer for 2¹/₂ hours. Stir the mixture every half hour during the freezing process. • Knead the marzipan with the rest of the icing sugar and add just enough maraschino liqueur to make a smooth mixture. • Add the remainder of the maraschino to the sorbet when next stirring. • Dust a work surface with icing sugar and roll out the marzipan until it is ¹/₂cm/¹/₄-inch thick. Cut six stars 8cm/3-inch diameter or circles 10cm/4-inch diameter, then cut these into stars. • Line six cups with cling film. Press the stars gently into the cups with the indentations curving upwards and place the cups in the freezer. • After freezing the sorbet for 2 hours, whisk the egg white until stiff and beat in the preserving sugar for two minutes. Fold the egg white into the cassis sorbet, which should be completely frozen and creamy, and freeze for a further 30 minutes. • Arrange the marzipan flowers on dessert plates and fill each with two small scoops or one large scoop of sorbet. • Pour two tbsps egg nog around each flower and pour the grenadine syrup over the egg nog. Mix the syrup and liqueur using a wooden skewer in a spiral motion and serve immediately.

Our Tip: Cassis, a French blackcurrant liqueur, can be used instead of maraschino. However, if this is too much alcohol surround the marzipan flowers with whipped cream instead of the egg nog and create the marbled effect with raspberry purée.

Tangy Sorbets

Both sorbets are well suited to serving as an interim course to clear the palate

Herb Sorbet
top left

1 tbsp each of finely chopped
fresh lemon balm, mint and dill

125ml/4 fl oz each of port and
water

Juice of 1 lemon

1 egg white

30g/1oz raw cane sugar

For decoration:

Small mint or lemon balm leaves

Preparation time: 15 minutes
Freezing time: 1 to 3 hours
Nutritional value:
Analysis per serving, approx:
• 290kJ/70kcal
• 3g protein
• 0g fat
• 8g carbohydrate

Process the chopped herbs, the port, water, lemon juice, egg white and raw cane sugar in a liquidiser or food processor for about 20 seconds. • Empty into a metal bowl, cover with aluminium foil and freeze for one to three hours until set. During this time, remove from the freezer at least once an hour, stir well to break up the ice crystals and return to the freezer. • Wash and pat dry the mint or lemon balm. • Spoon scoops of the sorbet onto plates and arrange the herbs around them or put the sorbet into wine glasses and decorate with the leaves.

Beetroot Sorbet
top right

1 small beetroot of about
100g/4oz

250ml/8 fl oz water

100g/4oz fresh pineapple chunks

50g/2oz honey

2 tbsps gin

Juice of 1 lemon

Grated rind of ½ lemon

1 egg white

Pinch of ground cloves

Fresh basil leaves or sprigs of
parsley to decorate

Preparation time: 20 minutes
Cooking: 15 minutes
Freezing time: 2 to 3 hours
Nutritional value:
Analysis per serving, approx:
• 375kJ/90kcal
• 4g protein
• 0g fat
• 17g carbohydrate

Wash, peel thinly and dice the beetroot. Put into a saucepan with a lid, cover, and simmer over low heat in the water for 15 minutes. Allow to cool. • Purée the pineapple in a liquidiser or food processor for about one minute with the cooled beetroot, the cooking liquid, the honey, gin, lemon juice and rind, the egg white and the cloves. • Place in a metal bowl, cover with aluminium foil and leave to set in the freezer for two to three hours. During the freezing time, stir well at least once an hour and return to the freezer. • Wash and dry the basil or parsley. • Scoop out portions of sorbet, place in wine glasses and decorate with the herbs.

Champagne Sorbet

An elegant summer party dessert; accompany with sponge fingers
An ice-cream maker is needed for this recipe

175g/6oz sugar
125ml/4 fl oz water
440 ml/15 fl oz chilled dry champagne or sparkling white wine
Juice of 1 large orange, chilled
100g/4oz wild strawberries
100g/4oz raspberries
1 large ripe peach
4 tbsps orange liqueur (Cointreau)
8 small leaves of mint or lemon balm

Preparation time: 30 minutes
Freezing time: 1½ hours
Nutritional value:
Analysis per serving, approx:
• 1590kJ/380kcal
• 2g protein
• 1g fat
• 67g carbohydrate

Boil the sugar and water in a heavy-based saucepan to make a clear syrup, stirring until the sugar has dissolved. Place the saucepan to cool over a bowl of water containing ice cubes. • Put the cooled sugar syrup, the well-chilled champagne and orange juice into an ice cream maker and follow the maker's instructions for freezing. • In the meantime, rinse the berries several times in a bowl of water and allow to drain. • Prick the peach several times with a fork, dip in boiling water, remove the skin, halve the fruit and remove the stone. • Dice the peach, mix with the berries and stir in the liqueur. Cover the fruit salad and marinate in the refrigerator. • Place four champagne glasses in the freezer. • Wash and dry the herbs. • Arrange scoops of sorbet in the champagne glasses and decorate with the herbs. • Pour the fruit salad and its marinade over the sorbets and serve at once.

Fine Fruit Granitas

These fruit-flavoured semi-frozen water ices are very refreshing

Peach Granita
top left

300g/10oz ripe peaches
Juice of $\frac{1}{2}$ lemon
3 tbsps light blossom honey
$\frac{1}{2}$ tsp vanilla essence
200ml/6 fl oz dry sparkling wine
3 dried peach halves to decorate

Preparation time: 20 minutes
Freezing time: 2 hours
Nutritional value:
Analysis per serving, approx:
- 750kJ/180kcal
- 1g protein
- 0g fat
- 34g carbohydrate

Prick the peaches with a fork in several places, dip quickly in boiling water and remove the skins. Halve the peaches, remove the stones and dice the flesh. • Place in a liquidiser or food processor with the lemon juice, honey, vanilla and dry sparkling wine, and purée for about one minute. • Place in a metal bowl, cover with aluminium foil and allow to set in the freezer for about two hours. Remove the purée from the freezer every half hour and stir thoroughly; then return it to the freezer. • Dice the dried peach halves very finely. • Serve scoops of the granita in dessert glasses and sprinkle with the diced peach.

Watermelon Granita
top right

1kg/2$\frac{1}{2}$lbs watermelon
3 tbsps lime juice
3 tsps icing sugar
For decoration:
4 leaves lemon balm, washed
4 tbsps well-chilled cherry brandy or gin

Preparation time: 30 minutes
Freezing time: 2 hours
Nutritional value:
Analysis per serving, approx:
- 545kJ/130kcal
- 2g protein
- 1g fat
- 18g carbohydrate

Cut the watermelon into wedges, peel them, remove the seeds and reserve two thin wedges in the refrigerator for decoration. • Dice the rest of the melon and purée in the liquidiser or food processor with the lime juice and icing sugar. Pour the melon purée into a shallow metal ice-cube tray or a loaf tin, cover with aluminium foil and freeze for two hours or until set. As soon as the purée begins to freeze along a strip about $\frac{1}{2}$cm/$\frac{1}{4}$-inch wide around the edges of the tray, stir carefully with a spoon so that the solid crystals mix with the liquid purée. Repeat this process several times until the purée has crystallised completely. • Spoon the water ice into four dessert dishes and decorate with the lemon balm leaves and the halved melon wedges. Sprinkle one tbsp cherry brandy or gin over each portion.

Lime Sorbet with Pinapple

An exquisite and decorative way of serving sorbet

1 pineapple weighing about 1 kg/2¹/₂lbs

4 tsps icing sugar

4 tbsps Maraschino

12 scoops of lime sorbet

25g/1oz each of coconut flakes, chopped pistachios and praline

150g/5¹/₂oz redcurrant jelly

Juice of ¹/₂ lime

Preparation time: 30 minutes
Marinating time: 2 hours
Nutritional value:
Analysis per serving, approx:
• 2180kJ/520kcal
• 5g protein
• 20g fat
• 54g carbohydrate

Cut a thin slice off the end of the pineapple with the leaf crown and set aside. • Peel the rest and cut into 1cm/¹/₂-inch thick rings. Remove the woody core from the rings. • Mix the icing sugar and Maraschino and sprinkle over the pineapple rings. Cover and leave to marinate in the refrigerator for two hours. • Put a large cake plate with raised edges or a ceramic flan dish into the freezer to become icy cold. • Roll four scoops of lime sorbet in the coconut flakes, four in the pistachios and four in the praline. Put back into the freezer to solidify again. • Arrange the pineapple rings on the cake plate. • Mix the redcurrant jelly with the lime juice and the marinade and place in the cool. Place scoops of the sorbet on the pineapple rings and around the plate. Decorate with the pineapple crown. Sprinkle the redcurrant sauce over the pineapple rings.

Our Tip: You can prepare the lime sorbet using the recipe for Champagne Sorbet, but replace the champagne with the juice of five limes and 250ml/8 fl oz white wine.

Citrons Givrés

This lemon water ice makes a refreshing dessert, givré means frosted or iced

Ingredients for 8 portions:

8 large, lemons

250ml/8 fl oz dry white wine

150g/5¹/₂oz sugar

1 egg white

Pinch of salt

50g/2oz candied lemon peel

2 tbsp orange liqueur

Preparation time: 30 minutes
Freezing time: 4¹/₂ hours
Nutritional value:
Analysis per serving, approx:
• 710kJ/170kcal
• 2g protein
• 5g fat
• 32g carbohydrate

Wash the lemons in warm water, dry them and cut a slice from the long side of each. Remove the flesh and wrap the empty skins and severed slices in aluminium foil and freeze. • Gently simmer the wine and sugar for five minutes, stirring, and allow to cool. • Remove the pith, pips and inner membranes from the lemon, but leave the fine skin between the segments as this provides extra taste. • Purée the flesh in a liquidiser or food processor. Mix with the cold wine, place in a metal bowl, cover with aluminium foil and leave to set in the freezer for four hours. • After nearly four hours whip the egg white with the salt until stiff. Dice the candied lemon peel finely and fold into the egg white with the liqueur. • Place the frozen fruit mixture in the liquidiser or food processor, grind finely then fold in the flavoured egg white. • Spoon the mixture into the lemon skins, top with a lid and place the lemons in the freezer for a further 30 minutes. • Remove the lemons from the freezer 15 minutes before serving.

Our Tip: The same dessert can be prepared using oranges or mandarins.

Ice Cream Gateau on a Meringue Base

This delicious concoction of ice cream set on a meringe base is perfect for celebrations

Ingredients for a 24cm/10-inch springform cake tin:

FOR THE MERINGUE BASE:

125ml/4 fl oz egg white (about 4 eggs)	
150g/5¹/₂oz caster sugar	
100g/4oz icing sugar	
2 tbsps cornflour	

FOR THE GATEAU:

100g/4oz sultanas	
125ml/4 fl oz rum	
1 tbsp lemon juice	
6 egg yolks	
100g/4oz icing sugar	
2 tbsps vanilla sugar	
¹/₂ vanilla pod	
1 l/1 ³/₄ pints whipping cream	
150g/5¹/₂oz plain chocolate	
100g/4oz coating chocolate	
50g/2oz chocolate shavings	

Preparation time: 1¹/₂ hours
Baking time: 3 hours
Freezing time: 5 hours

Nutritional value:

Analysis per serving (serves 12):

- 2730kJ/650kcal
- 14g protein
- 38g fat
- 44g carbohydrate

Whisk the egg whites until stiff and continue whisking while slowly adding the caster sugar until glossy. Sift the icing sugar and cornflour over the egg whites and fold in with a metal spoon. • Heat the oven to 100°C/212°F/Gas Mark ¹/₄. Line a baking sheet with baking parchment. • Place the cake tin on the baking sheet and trace its shape with a pencil. • Put the meringue into a piping bag with a star nozzle and fill in the marked circle with a spiral of meringue. • Place on the middle shelf of the oven and dry, rather than bake, for three hours. Keep the oven door ajar with the handle of a wooden spoon. • Wash the sultanas in hot water and drain them. Pour rum and lemon juice over the sultanas. • Beat the egg yolks with the icing sugar and vanilla sugar until white and fluffy. • Split the vanilla pod lengthways, scrape out the inside and mix into the egg yolk mixture. • Beat 600ml/18 fl oz cream until stiff and fold half of it into the vanilla mixture. Place this in the spring form tin and place in the freezer. • Break the chocolate and the coating chocolate into pieces and melt together over a pan of simmering water, stirring in 200ml/6 fl oz un-whipped cream. Cool and add the rum from the sultanas and the rest of the whipped cream. • Arrange the sultanas on the vanilla ice cream and spread the chocolate cream on top. • Whip the rest of the cream until stiff and place in a piping bag with a star nozzle. • Loosen the edge of the gateau with a knife, hold the base of the mould briefly over steam, remove sides of the tin and slide the ice cream gateau onto the cold meringue base. Mark 12 portions on the gateau. Decorate each with a garland of cream and the chocolate shavings. • Keep the gateau in the freezer until it is to be served.

Important Dessert Ingredients

There is no substitute for good quality fresh fruit in the preparation of desserts. Fresh fruit is also an important part of a balanced diet. It provides carbohydrates, minerals and vitamins in quantities significant for dietary needs. As many types of fruit have a water content of 80 to 85 percent, the calorie count is not very high.

An abundance of different fresh fruit is available the whole year round. However, it is best to use whatever fruit is in season at the particular time. Its taste is then at its best and it is not as expensive. Exotic fruits enrich the range of desserts, especially in winter. Berries and stone-fruits are generally only available for a brief period, but apples are on sale the whole year round. However apricots, peeled apples and pears, cherries, peaches, plums, greengages, damsons, rhubarb and berries, as well as pineapple, grapefruit, oranges, guavas and kiwi fruits can all be frozen.

Pineapple

Season: all year round.
The pineapple grows on a bush 80 to 100-cm (about three to four feet) high and is cultivated throughout the tropics. It tastes fruitily sweet and sharp. The ripe fruit has a strong smell and its golden-brown, thorny rind should give slightly when pressed at the stalk end. Never buy an unripe pineapple, this is one of the few fruits that do not ripen further after picking. The best way to peel a pineapple is shown in the introduction.

Pineapple is used in many ways in a great variety of meat dishes, snacks, cocktails, desserts and fruit salads. It also makes an exquisite dessert on its own, cut into slices, flavoured with a little cognac and decorated with whipped cream. Miniature pineapples are an extra small, very tasty new type with a thinner rind. They are grown mostly on the Ivory Coast.

Passion fruit

(maracuja, grenadilla)
Season: from August to April.
Passion fruit comes from Eastern and South Africa, Taiwan, South America, California and Australia. There are two varieties, one with yellow skin, the other with purple skin. Both have a yellow pulp containing many small seeds which are eaten with the fruit. The fruit has a strong fragrance which is reminiscent of strawberries or apricots. If the tough skin of this plum-like fruit is wrinkled, the passion fruit will still taste good but should be eaten fairly soon. To do so, cut it open and spoon out the jelly-like flesh.

Kiwi fruit

Season: the entire year.
This fruit is about the size of a hens egg, with juicy green flesh and brown, hairy skin. It comes mostly from New Zealand but is also grown in California, Spain and France. When the fruit gives under finger pressure it is fully ripe. Hard kiwi fruits will ripen a little at room temperature and can be stored for up to two weeks. Ripe kiwi fruits should be stored in the refrigerator until eaten. Kiwi fruits are particularly rich in Vitamin C and very low in calories. Peeled and cut into slices or wedges, they can be used in a variety of ways.

Cape gooseberry

(Physalis)
Season: from December to July.
Cape gooseberries come from Peru and South Africa but are now grown in all parts of the tropics. The greenish-yellow to bright yellow berries are encased in a papery husk which is the plant calyx. They are eaten fresh or are prepared like other soft fruits. They taste sweet-sour and make a subtle addition to salads and are especially attractive as a cake decoration with the husks folded back. They are particularly rich in vitamin C.

Gooseberry

Season: from June to August.
Gooseberries are native to Europe and North Africa. Ripe gooseberries are yellow-green, pink to light brown, and some types are hairy, whilst others are smooth. Jams, preserves and fruit fools are made from the green and unripe gooseberries; fully ripe gooseberries should be eaten raw as fresh as possible. Gooseberries are traditionally made into a sharp sauce to serve with mackerel.

Mango

Season: throughout the year.
Mangoes can weigh up to three kg and are the fruit of the Indian mango tree. They are now cultivated in all tropical regions. The mango is shaped like a pear or kidney and has a greenish-red rind which can be scored with a sharp knife and then peeled off. The juicy, golden-yellow flesh has to be cut away from the stone in wedges. When the fruit is ripe the strong aroma is fruity and sweet. Mangoes can be used in a variety of ways to make fruit salads, cream desserts and gâteaux. They also taste good with poultry, cheese or ham.

Papaya

(Pawpaw)
Season: from October to June.
The greenish-yellow, pear-shaped fruits give slightly to pressure when fully ripe and have bright, orange-red flesh. The black seeds are peppery and can be used as flavouring in salads. Originally from South America, they are now grown in all tropical and subtropical regions.

Pineapple

Miniature pineapple

Passion fruit

Kiwi

Papaya

Mango

Cape gooseberries (physalis)

Gooseberries

Figs

Fruits from all over the world

Papayas are very easily digestible thanks to an enzyme they contain and are often eaten for breakfast in hot countries. They are rich in Vitamin A. Papayas are suitable for fruit salads, cream desserts, as a garnish for cold platters or, when briefly fried in butter, as an accompaniment for meat.

Fig

Season: from June to November, less frequently available in other months.
Originally from Asia Minor, the evergreen fig tree is today grown around the Mediterranean, in South Africa, California and South America. Fresh figs weigh from 50 to 70g (2-3 oz) and taste sweet. They should be eaten as soon as possible after purchase. Some types of fig have a yellowish skin, while in others the skin is blueish-green to violet. Ripe figs are soft and the skin must be neither blemished nor sticky.
Fresh figs are eaten raw, whether peeled or not, and can be sprinkled with a little cognac. However, they also taste good when combined with wine or vanilla custard, in fruit salads, with ham, smoked fish and above all with fresh goat's cheese.

Persimmon

(Kaki, Sharon fruit)
Season: from November to March.
These are the fruits of an East Asian ebony tree now grown in southern Europe, North America and Brazil. Persimmon are an orange-red colour; when ripe they become soft and slightly darker. In shape they resemble large tomatoes.
This fruit contains tannin and is bitter and has an unpleasantly 'furry' taste in the mouth when unripe. Persimmons are especially rich in vitamin A. Their aroma is reminiscent of apricots and peaches. Sharon fruit, a new strain of persimmon from the Plain of Sharon in Israel, are free of tannin and therefore also taste good when firm. The smaller, light orange fruits are in season between March and May.

Apricot

Season: from May to September.
These orange-yellow stone-fruits related to the plum, with their slightly bitter smell and velvety skin have a high vitamin A content. Apricots originally came from China and do well in all sunny climates. They will continue to ripen a little at room temperature and can be stored for two to three days. Fruits which are not quite ripe are also suitable for compote or for jam-making.
When they are to be eaten fresh they must be completely ripe.

Peach

Season: from May to September.
Peaches are mainly cultivated in southern Europe and California. The apple-size fruit with the velvety skin has a hard stone which encloses an oil-bearing seed. The whitish or golden flesh is juicy and has an aromatic sweetness. When hard, the fruits are not quite ripe but will ripen a little at room temperature; when fully ripe they should be kept for two days at the most, stored in the refrigerator. When used in desserts they are usually peeled; to do this, scald the fruit in hot or boiling water for two minutes; then the skin will pull off easily. Peaches are delicious either served with ice cream or in drinks such as fruit cups or champagne.

Nectarine

Season: from May to August.
A smooth skinned variety of peach. The skin is red and yellow, smooth and shiny.
Nectarines are grown in Japan, California and South Africa as well as in the countries of southern Europe.
Even when fully ripe, nectarines have a fairly firm flesh; soft fruits are over-ripe and will spoil quickly.

Melon

Melons belong to the squash family. There is a basic distinction between sweet melons and watermelons. Sweet melon varieties include musk, honeydew, cantaloupe and ogen. Honeydew melons have a yellow-green to orange-red, honey-sweet flesh. Ripe fruits smell aromatic. Muskmelons have a network pattern on their skin. Cantaloupe melons are greenish-yellow and can be the size of a football, their flesh is apricot-coloured and tastes particularly spicy. Watermelons have a dark green or pale green skin and bright red flesh with lots of dark seeds. However some new varieties have white, yellow or orange flesh. Melons are about 95 percent water. A ripe watermelon sounds hollow when tapped on the outside.

Plum

Season: from July to October
There are so many varieties of plum and it is difficult to tell the spherical and egg-shaped stone-fruits apart. Among this large family there are large, round, blueish-violet Victoria plums as well as round, red egg-plums, small yellow mirabelles, greenish-yellow greengages and oval, purple damson plums. The taste varies from sweet to sour

Watermelon

Muskmelon

Sharon fruit (persimmon)

Peach

Apricots

Strawberries

Nectarine

Honeydew melon

Red, yellow and purple plums

Wild strawberries

Raspberries

Important Dessert Ingredients

depending on the type. When buying, choose plums with dry but not wrinkled skin. The early types are suitable for eating raw because the flesh is softer. For cake-making, jam-making and freezing use later types, particularly damsons. These are more suitable, as they contain more fruit sugar and less water than the other plums.

Cherry
Season: from May to August
There are many varieties of cherry, which vary in colour from yellow to red to black. Sweet cherries, which are eaten raw, include varieties such as the red-black Bing and white cherries (usually pale yellow) like Queen Anne or Napoleon. Sour cherries, such as the Morello and Amarello, are used in cooking to make pies, jams and flambées.

Strawberry
(Illustrated previous page)
Season: from late May to July.
Of the many different varieties of cultivated strawberry the small, dark red ones have the most aromatic flavour. Genuine wild strawberries are rarely on sale, and then only in small quantities. When buying strawberries, look out for ripe, dry fruits with no bruising. If possible, they should be eaten on the day of purchase.

Raspberry
(Illustrated previous page)
Season: from June to September.

The tender raspberry grows wild in all temperate climates. Wild raspberries have more flavour than garden varieties. The conical or round berries taste sweet and aromatic and are made into jam and preserves, jelly, juice, syrup and ice cream. Fresh raspberries must be added to a fruit salad at the last possible moment because of their susceptibility to bruising, and if possible they should be eaten on the day of purchase. For storage, they should be spread out on a tray in a cool place.

Blackberry
Season: from July to October.
The blue-black shiny berries grow wild at the edges of heaths and woods and are cultivated in gardens. Wild blackberries are smaller with more seeds but have more flavour. In contrast to raspberries, blackberries only separate from the stalk easily when fully ripe.

Bilberry
(blueberry, whortleberry)
Season: from July to September.
These dull blue, sweet-and-sour berries grow wild in woods and on moorland, especially on high ground. They are very rich in vitamin C and taste best when freshly picked, sprinkled with sugar and served with a topping of whipped cream. Cultivated bilberries are larger

but cannot compete with the wild variety for taste.

Redcurrant, blackcurrant, whitecurrant
Season: from June to August.
Redcurrants, blackcurrants and whitecurrants grow on bushes which are native to parts of Europe and Asia. Redcurrants taste sharp and sour, the black ones are somewhat bitter. Blackcurrants have the highest vitamin C content of all the berries and also supply a great deal of potassium. Whitecurrants are rarely sold commercially and deteriorate very quickly.

Grape
Season: all year round.
Grapes are imported from as far afield as Greece, France, Chile, Argentina and South Africa. Eighty-five percent of the grape harvest is used to make wine, and five percent is dried and sold as raisins, sultanas and currants. Only ten percent are sold as table grapes. Dessert grapes are blue-black, yellow or green and have a fairly thin skin. The pips and skins are roughage which stimulate the digestive process. The high glucose content makes the sweet berries rich in calories. Muscatel is a variety which tastes a little of nutmeg and is also made into raisins. Reginas are a particularly sweet variety of black grape which is harvested from mid-August.

Orange
Season: from November to June, sometimes at other times of the year.
The orange is a fruit redolent of warmer climes. Oranges are imported from Spain, Israel and Morocco during the winter and from South Africa, Argentina and Brazil during the summer. The colour of the rind is no indication of the quality. Oranges with a pale rind are just as ripe as those which are orange-red. The colour is the only distinction between blond and blood oranges. Navel oranges are a bright orange colour, seedless and mild-flavoured. Green oranges, sometimes known as Cuban oranges, are perfectly ripe; they come from the Caribbean. If orange rind is to be grated or used as a julienne, buy oranges which have not been sprayed.

Mandarin
(Tangerine)
Season: from October to February.
The mandarine is a collective name for a group of small citrus fruits with sweet, aromatic flesh, pips and a thin peel which is easily detachable.
Satsumas are an early variety, which have hardly any pips and originate from Japan, though they are imported from North Africa. Clementines are a cross between

Blood orange

Grapefruit

Seville Orange

Mandarins

Grapes

Cherries

Redcurrants

Fruits from all over the world

the tangerine and the Seville orange, and are on sale from November to January; they originated in Algeria but are imported from other citrus-growing areas. Mandarins originally came from China but are now grown on Java, Sumatra, in southern Europe and Israel.

Grapefruit
Season: October to May, less easy to find during other months but nearly always available.
The grapefruit is a spontaneous cross between a citron (a thick-skinned citrus fruit which is no longer grown commercially) and a lemon. The yellow to pinkish-red fruit flesh, almost devoid of pips, tastes fruity and tangy but is also sour and bitter. Pink and ruby-red-fleshed grapefruits are identical in flavour to the yellow ones. Grapefruit originated in the Caribbean. It is now imported from the USA, Israel, Spain and Africa.

Banana
Season: the entire year.
Bananas are among the oldest cultivated fruits and mainly come from the West Indies, Central and South America, the Canaries and Africa. The banana bush has long, flat leaves and a large,

tulip-shaped flower. When it fruits, it puts out 8 to 14 'hands' of bananas consisting of up to 20 bananas each. The fruit is ready for harvesting after about three-and-a-half months. The creamy fruit flesh of the fruit contains little fruit acid. As the banana ripens, the starch is converted to sugar; it then becomes soft and sweet. Small brown freckles on the skin indicate ripeness. It is best to buy bananas when ripe but still firm. They can then be kept at room temperature for at least a week. As bananas tend to turn brown shortly after peeling, the fruit should be sprinkled with lemon juice immediately. Sliced bananas are added to fruit salads; they may also be halved and fried in butter, or flambéed or puréed, and they are used in creamy desserts.

Apple
Season: available throughout the year due to their good keeping qualities.
In pre-Christian times at least three types of wild apple were known. Today there are innumerable varieties which are classified according to set quality standards. Dessert or eating apples are those of the best

quality. Organically grown apples are generally more blemished in appearance, but mostly compensate for this with a better flavour.
The types of apple most commonly grown in Britain are Cox's Orange Pippin, Worcester Pearmain, Golden Delicious and Bramley. Other varieties are found occasionally, such as Russet. Apples imported from Europe include Golden Delicious, Red Delicious and Jonathan. Granny Smiths and Newtowns come from Australia, South Africa and the U.S.A. Rome Beauty and Washington are red-skinned apples imported from the northwestern United States. Our recipes commonly recommend Bramley's or Cox's Orange Pippin. The Bramley is a classic cooking apple, large and with a strong, sour flavour. Cox's Orange Pippin contains very fine fruit acids and is therefore best eaten in fruit salads or other fresh fruit composite desserts.
Other types of apple, as well as those which do not meet the quality standards for fresh fruit, are processed into apple purée or sauce. To produce thickened apple syrup, apple juice is boiled with little or no sugar, until thick. Apples have traditionally been fermented to make cider and apple brandy (applejack or Calvados). Cider apples are small and bitter and not eaten raw.

Pear
Season: from August to October
Pears are imported from South Africa in March and April and from the U.S.A. During the season they are home-grown or come from elsewhere in Europe. Pears have very little fruit acid and therefore they mostly taste sweeter than apples. Their high potassium content gives them a dehydrating effect. The most important types of pear are Comice, Conference and Sweet William. Pears are stewed for desserts in a little red or white wine or eaten raw, often peeled. Dried pears are stewed for desserts or used like raisins in baking. A liqueur called William is also made from pears.

Rhubarb
Season: from January to June. Rhubarb originates from Northern Asia. In olden times the root of the 'barbaric' (foreign) plant was used as a laxative. Rhubarb first became popular as a stewed fruit in Holland in the mid-nineteenth century. The reddish, juicy, fleshy stalks of the bushy plant taste fruity and sharp. Like the melon or pumpkin, rhubarb is really a vegetable, in botanical terms, but like fruit can be made into jam, preserves or compote and can be used in cake-making. Before cooking, all the leaves must be discarded as they are poisonous. Trim off the end of the stalk and the tough, outer stringy skin, and cut into chunks. Stew in a little water with lemon juice and sugar. Raw stalks can be kept for one to two days in the refrigerator without loss of quality.
The most important thing to remember when preparing desserts is that the flavours must complement each other. This is

Rhubarb

Bananas

Pears, various varieties

Cox's Orange Pippin

Golden Delicious

Worcester Apple

Blackberries

Bilberries

Important Dessert Ingredients

really an art; the quantities and combinations must be carefully measured and the main ingredient must not be overwhelmed by the lesser ones.

Some of the flavourings most often used in desserts are described below. Alcohol is often included as it is useful for enhancing the flavours of the other ingredients.

Alcohol in moderation

It is entirely proper to use alcohol to flavour desserts, and the quantities used are so small that the alcohol consumption is hardly significant. What is more, when cooked, the alcoholic content evaporates, leaving only the flavour behind. Spirits are particularly compatible with fruits when used in desserts. Some of the wines and liqueurs used in the recipes in this book are listed below, and alternatives are also given when they are hard to find.

Alchermes, Italian herbal liqueur; use vermouth or other herbal liqueurs
Amaretto, Italian almond liqueur; use maraschino or kirsch instead
Calvados, apple brandy from Normandy; use Drambuie instead
Cassis, French blackcurrant liqueur
Cognac, brandy from the French region of the same name
Cointreau, liqueur from the rind of bitter oranges
Egg liqueur, a drink

made from egg yolks, sugar and brandy (egg nog or advocaat)
Grand Marnier, an orange-flavoured liqueur based on cognac; Curaçao or Triple Sec can be used instead
Madeira, a sweet, heavy wine named after the Portuguese island in the Atlantic; any sweet wine, such as Alicante or Commandaria can be used instead
Maraschino, cherry liqueur from Italy and Yugoslavia; can be replaced by cherry brandy
Rum, spirit made from sugar cane; imported from the Caribbean
Sherry, a fortified dessert wine, originally from Spain, now also produced in Australia, Cyprus and South Africa

Honey

Beekeeping was a flourishing art in Egypt 4,000 years ago. Until the introduction of cane sugar, honey from the bee was the only sweetener available in Europe. There are two types, blossom honey from nectar (for example: acacia, heather, clover and linden honey) and honeydew honey made from other parts of the plant (for example: leaf, pine and spruce honey).

Honey breaks down in the human body in the same way that ordinary sugar does and has a similar calorie content. Overheating removes the healthy active agents in honey. Honey can be stored for up to one year.

Maple syrup

This is one of the alternative sweeteners used in wholefood cooking. It is the sap of the maple, a broad-leaved, deciduous North American tree. It was originally tapped from the extensive maple forests of North America by the native peoples. As sugar was a rarity, maple syrup became one of the staple foods. Today it is still made from the sap of maple trees growing in Canada and the United States. In its native countries the syrup is also dried and made into granules called maple sugar. During the four- to six-week annual harvest in March and April, the composition of the juice changes. It loses the concentrated sweetness which it has at the beginning and the mineral content increases. To produce 1 litre (1 3/4 pints) of syrup, 40 to 50 litres (70

to 80 pints) of natural maple juice are used.

Once the container has been opened, maple syrup should be kept in a cool place and should be used as soon as possible.

Raw cane sugar

A newly rediscovered, alternative method of sweetening. Raw cane sugar, not to be confused with demerara sugar, is the dried, unrefined juice of organically-grown cane sugar. All the nutrients and trace elements are retained through the gentle milling process unlike white and demerara sugars which have had all the valuable nutrients refined out of them. Both light and dark raw cane sugar is available and the malty taste, reminiscent of liquorice or treacle, is more marked in the dark sugar. If you are not used to the taste try the lighter type first.

Raw cane sugar does not sweeten as much as white sugar, but it is generally felt to have a fuller flavour.

Ginger

Ginger varies in flavour from spicy and sharp to slightly sweet. The gnarled roots of this reed-like bush are now grown in almost all tropical countries. The popularity of Far Eastern cuisine has made ginger a 'hot' item; this is a good thing as it had been largely forgotten in European cuisine. The thicker parts of the root are

Red wine

White wine

Egg liqueur

Sherry

Rum

Cognac

Alchermes liqueur

Honey

Cloves

Nut spread

Ginger in syrup

Crystallised ginger

Cinnamon sticks

Vanilla pods

Delicate Aromas

mostly sold in crystallised form; the finger-thin lateral roots, peeled or unpeeled, are cut into pieces or ground. The young lateral shoots (stem ginger) are sold preserved in syrup. The unusual flavour of ginger goes well with sweet and/or spicy dishes.

Cloves
These dried flower buds are available whole or in ground form. They have a very strong flavour and smell like carnations. The spicy buds, used since the Middle Ages, come from the Moluccan island of Ambon, and from Madagascar and Zanzibar. It is said that oil of cloves has a fortifying effect on the stomach, liver and heart. Certainly it is an effective remedy for toothache. Apart from fruit desserts, cloves can be used as a spice in gingerbread, apple tart, sweet-and-sour vegetable pickles and punch or mulled wine. Cloves lose their potency if stored for too long.

Cinnamon
For centuries, cinnamon has been a sought-after spice, the best quality coming from Sri Lanka. Cinnamon is the dried inner bark of the cinnamon tree, which rolls up to form what is sold as cinnamon sticks. The more spicy Cassia bark relative is usually ground into a powder. Cinnamon is a strong spice and should be used sparingly.

Vanilla
Genuine vanilla is available as vanilla essence, in vanilla sugar and as whole vanilla pods. The pods are about 20cm/8 inches long and blackish-brown in colour. To use the pods, split them and scrape out the inside. Vanilla sugar can be made quite simply from the pods. Place normal white granulated or caster sugar in a screw-top jar, split a vanilla pod in half and add it to the jar and close tightly. If a creamy mixture is being made in the liquidizer or food processor, it can be flavoured by grinding a piece of vanilla pod with it.

Chocolate
A silky, unblemished gloss on chocolate indicates that it is of high quality. The main ingredients are cocoa mass, cocoa butter, sugar and powdered milk or cream. Soya lecithin, used as an emulsifying agent, makes the chocolate mixture smoother.
To melt chocolate, put it in a basin and heat it over a pan of simmering water, or grate it for creamy desserts. An excellent way to melt chocolate is to put it in a plastic container and heat it in the microwave oven for three minutes at the lowest setting. Chocolate decorations can be made easily at home, although they may also be bought in many different shapes and forms.

Nut spread
This confection consists of finely ground hazelnuts or almonds, caramelised sugar, coating chocolate and cocoa butter. It is also easy to make at home.

Marzipan
Marzipan is a confection made from a very high proportion of almonds and not more than 35 percent sugar. It is a high quality commercial product and saves the cook a great deal of work. To make your own marzipan, combine ground almonds with icing sugar and a few drops of orange flower or rosewater and knead well.

Rosewater
A drop of rose oil will give a lasting perfume to 250ml/8fl oz water. Like orange flower water, rosewater is used for flavouring subtle desserts, sweet pastries or home-made marzipan.

Orange flower water
This is made by distilling fresh, closed flower-buds of the orange and other citrus trees. Like rosewater, it can be bought in healthfood shops.

Orange juice
Use either home-made or bought freshly-squeezed juice, as long-life juice has a somewhat inadequate flavour.

Buckthorn juice
This unusual juice is made from the yellow-red berries which are rich in Vitamin C. It is imported from the Continent. Unsweetened buckthorn juice found in healthfood shops is often used in wholefood cooking. Blackcurrant juice or rose-hip syrup can be substituted but you may have to reduce the sugar content.

Grenadine
Grenadine is the juice of the pomegranate which is heavily sweetened and thickened to a syrup. Pomegranates are grown in the Mediterranean and the sub-tropics. The syrup is also used to flavour cocktails. It is a clear, pale red colour and imparts a very attractive pink to creamy desserts.

Grape juice

Maple syrup

Grenadine

Orange juice

Root ginger

Marzipan

Chocolate

Rosewater

Orange flower water

Buckthorn juice

Vanilla powder

Raw cane sugar

Making Ice Cream

Hot Tips for Frozen Desserts

Home-made ice cream can be made in a number of ways. It is characterised above all by the quality of its ingredients and unlike many commercial ice creams it contains no thickening agents, artificial emulsifiers, artificial flavourings and colourings.

When making home-made ice cream, the freshest ingredients are of prime importance. A basic mixture of egg yolks and cream with a 30 percent fat content guarantees a delicious ice cream. The addition of sugar and alcohol prevent the ice cream from freezing too hard. If you are starting to experiment with ice cream recipes there is no need to buy an expensive ice cream making machine at first. It is perfectly possible to produce excellent ice cream without one though it does take much longer to freeze. The mixture should be transferred to a metal container and will need between two and five hours in the freezer. It should be stirred with a spatula every hour or so, to stop large fromcrystals forming. The stirring may be omitted in the case of light, fluffy mixtures containing a lot of egg yolk or cream. Sorbets or granitas made of sweetened fruit juices or purée, to which very little or no alcohol has been added, should be stirred every 30 minutes. The main advantage of working with an ice cream maker is that it does the stirring for you and the ice cream should be ready in 20 to 30 minutes.

The following basic rules should be followed when preparing ice cream:

• Cleanliness and hygiene are of particular importance to prevent any bacterial contamination of the ingredients.

• The temperature of the freezer must be 18°C/0°F. Ensure that the door of the freezer is only opened briefly for stirring purposes.

• The basic ingredients, such as eggs, cream and milk should be as fresh as possible. Long-life milk or cream spoils the taste of ice cream, and UHT cream will not whip as stiffly as fresh cream.

• The egg-yolk-and-sugar mixture must be beaten over a pan of hot water until thick and creamy, then cooled down over a pan of cold water. Egg whites and whipped cream must both be beaten until very stiff before being carefully folded into the other ingredients.

• The ice cream mixture must be placed in the freezer or ice cream maker directly after mixing. At room temperature the light, foamy mixture collapses quickly.

• Strongly flavoured fruits, lightly roasted nuts, genuine vanilla, chocolate, nougat or marzipan, and sweet alcoholic drinks all make good ice cream flavourings. For sweetening, use caster or raw cane sugar or the various types of honey. Remember that ice cream needs more sweetening than other desserts.

• For sorbets, ring the changes by using vegetables such as cucumber, beetroot, tomato or courgettes. Or try finely chopped fresh herbs, slightly sweetened. The results can be served as a refreshing intermediate course or appetiser at an elegant dinner party or as a light dessert.

• If freezing without an ice cream maker, always put the ice cream mixture in a metal bowl as metal is a better conductor than say plastic. To ensure a creamy consistency, the ice cream must be stirred every hour to break down the ice crystals which form round edges of the bowl.

• If your ice cream maker uses ice cubes and salt in the traditional way, be sure to have an adequate supply of ice cubes on hand in the freezer. You can now buy bags of ice cubes from large super-markets.

• Ice cream made from fresh ingredients can be kept for several weeks. However, it tastes best if eaten soon after it is made or certainly within one week. Put the ice cream in airtight plastic containers before storing in the freezer.

• Ice cream which has been kept in the freezer is usually too hard to eat immediately. Transfer it to the refrigerator 30 minutes before serving so that it can easily be scooped out. It also tastes better if it is not too cold. Thawed ice cream should on no account be refrozen.

Mixing bowls

Bombe mould

Electric hand-held blender

Cassata mould

Ice cream scoops

Special steel ice cream dishes

Useful Equipment

A measuring jug and/or kitchen scales and an electric hand-beater are really essential. A food processor or liquidiser is also useful although some recipes require only a balloon whisk. Metal mixing bowls speed up the process when making ice cream without an ice cream maker.

A bombe mould with a lid, or other ice cream moulds, such as the cassata mould shown below, also made of metal, should form part of a well-equipped kitchen. If you do not have any, a similarly shaped glass mixing bowl should be used for ice creams which are to be unmoulded.

You will need a spatula to stir the ice cream mixture during the freezing process and some plastic containers for storage. Stainless steel ice cream scoops in various sizes, when dipped in cold water, make it possible to form beautiful balls of ice cream. With a roll-type scoop you can scrape long strips off the surface of the ice cream. In this type, the handle is filled with glycerine and thus transfers warmth from your hand to the spoon; this makes it relatively easy to serve even hard-frozen ice cream.

Spaghetti ice cream, which is especially popular with children, is made by pressing vanilla ice cream through a potato ricer or noodle maker directly into a chilled dessert bowl. A sauce of strained raspberry purée and a sprinkling of grated coconut can be made to look very similar to tomato sauce and grated Parmesan!

Ice cream will melt a little more slowly if you serve it in classic, well-chilled metal sundae dishes.

Which Ice Cream Maker Should You Buy?

The system for making ice cream is identical in all ice cream makers. A mixture is prepared and stirred constantly at a low temperature until the ice cream is ready. There is quite a wide choice of machines. The prices and designs vary and there are both hand operated and electrically driven models. Both types consist of a container into which the ice cream or sorbet mixture is poured. In the manually operated machine there is a stirring handle in the lid. The tightly closed drum containing the ice cream is placed in a larger container and the space between is filled with ice cubes, 250g-500g/8oz-16oz of the cheapest cooking salt and a little iced water. The handle is then turned by hand for 20 to 30 minutes until the ice cream stiffens. Electric machines have a motor which stops automatically when the ice cream is stiff enough to resist the motor. At this point, the ice cream is frozen to a creamy consistency and is ready to eat.

Some $1\frac{1}{4}$-$1\frac{1}{2}$ litres/2-$2\frac{1}{2}$ pints of ice cream can be prepared at once. To make several flavours you will need a large stock of ice cubes. With the latest models of ice cream maker it is no longer necessary to use ice cubes or salt. The correct temperature is produced by a coolant which is already contained in the drum of the machine. The drum is kept in the freezer for at least seven hours at -18°C/0°F, then it is filled with the ice cream mixture and attached to the motor. As in the classic type of ice cream maker, the ice cream is made whilst being constantly stirred. The drum is cold enough to make two successive batches of ice cream. With this type of machine, it is also important to remove the ice cream from the metal drum to a plastic container for storage in the freezer because later the hard ice cream will be difficult to scrape out of the drum without scratching it.

An ice cream maker with its own integral refrigeration unit is the most expensive type. Minimal preparation is required to convert the basic custard mixture to ice cream using this type of machine.

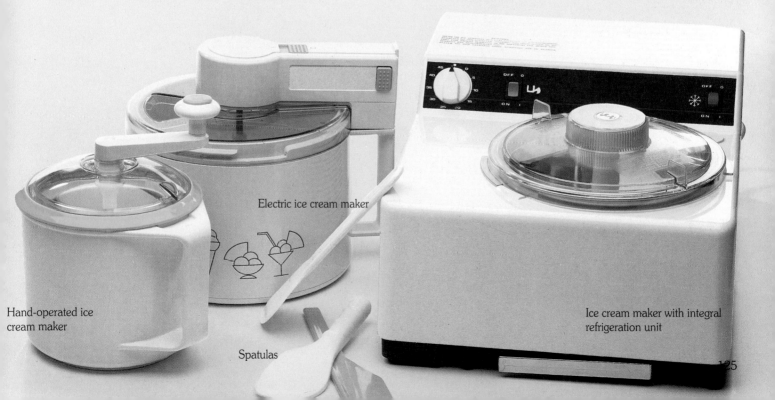

Hand-operated ice cream maker

Electric ice cream maker

Spatulas

Ice cream maker with integral refrigeration unit

Index

Index